T0302983

CONVERSATIONS WITH ROSSINI

By Richard Osborne

Rossini
Conversations with Karajan
Herbert von Karajan: A Life in Music
Till I End my Song
Garsington Opera: A Celebration
The Grange, Hampshire
Music and Musicians of Eton

FERDINAND HILLER

Conversations with Rossini

―――――

TRANSLATED AND ANNOTATED
WITH AN INTRODUCTION BY

Richard Osborne

PALLAS ATHENE

Rossini has the drollest, most amusing things to say about Paris and all the musicians there, and about himself and his compositions; and he speaks of all contemporaries with such tremendous respect that one might take him quite literally, if one had no eyes to see the sly expression on his face. But all his looks and words are full of wit and liveliness and intelligence, and anyone who denies his genius would certainly recant on hearing him holding forth like this.

Felix Mendelssohn, letter to his mother and sister, 14 July 1836

Ferdinand Hiller

Introduction

The conversations which took place between the 63-year-old Gioachino Rossini (1792–1868) and Ferdinand Hiller (1811–1885) in Trouville in Normandy in September 1855, and the finely drawn impression of Rossini with which Hiller prefaces the conversations, are of more than usual interest. No other single source offers so vivid a sense of Rossini the man and the musician.

The meeting was timely. That summer Rossini and his second wife Olympe had returned to Paris after a 17-year Italian residency in Bologna and Florence during which a series of debilitating physical and depressive illnesses had brought Rossini's creative life to a virtual standstill. The move proved to be highly efficacious. Between 1855 and his death in 1868, Rossini enjoyed improved health and a new urge to compose. The days he spent with Hiller in Trouville in September 1855 marked the start of Rossini's own Indian summer.

Rossini first met Hiller at Lionel Rothschild's house in Paris is 1828. Hiller, who had just celebrated his 17th birthday, clearly delighted Rossini. 'You're the most cheerful fellow I've ever met,' quipped the Maestro. 'After the Pope, that is.' The son of a wealthy Jewish merchant, Hiller would have entered one of the learned professions had his musical gifts not won plaudits from the likes of Spohr, Moscheles and, more particularly, his young teenage friend Felix Mendelssohn. It was on Mendelssohn's recommendation that the 14-year-old Hiller moved to Weimar to study with the pianist and composer Johann Nepomuk Hummel. By the time Rossini made Hiller's acquaintance in 1828, the boy had already played privately for Goethe and travelled with Hummel to Vienna to visit the dying Beethoven.

Rossini and Hiller remained in Paris until the mid-1830s. In 1829 Hiller gave the French première of Beethoven's Fifth Piano Concerto. The concert, conducted by François-Antoine Habeneck who had recently conducted the première of Rossini's *Guillaume Tell*, also included works by the 25-year-old Hector Berlioz. Berlioz became a friend of Hiller with whom he shared an attachment to the beautiful but vixenish Camille Moke, the 'celestial pianofortist' as Thomas De Quincey called her. Berlioz sought Hiller's advice on the redrafting of the third movement of the *Symphonie Fantastique* but it was Hiller's gifts as a listener and confidant – gifts Rossini himself would later value – that most commended him to Berlioz.

Robert Schumann, whose world-renowned A minor Piano Concerto is dedicated to Hiller, said of Hiller's compositions, 'For all his formal mastery, his music lacks that triumphant power which we are unable to resist'. Hiller was, however, a fine all-round musician, as well as a much-admired pianist. As late as 1871 *The Musical Times* wrote, 'This incomparable artist reproduces a method which was born and nurtured in the days of pure music, when phrasing and expression came from the heart through the fingers, and digital dexterity was reserved for its legitimate use'. No wonder Rossini admired his playing.

In Dresden in the mid-1840s Hiller's home been a gathering-place for artists and intellectuals. It was there that Schumann heard Wagner read the libretto of *Lohengrin* for the first time; Chopin and Liszt were friends, as was the revolutionary Russian Mikhail Bakunin. (Unlike Rossini, Hiller was always somewhat to the left politically.)

Rossini, like Hiller, was a man of wide cultural experience who knew at first-hand an astonishing amount of music, much of it from memory. The two men had also met an extraordinary array of people. Rossini's list included kings, tsars and politicians, as well as singers, instrumentalists and fellow composers, all remembered with that keen eye and ready wit for which he was famous. It is not surprising, therefore, that the conversations are remarkably wide-ranging. Responding with alacrity to Hiller's shrewdly placed questions, Rossini is more than happy to engage with subjects as abstruse as the aesthetics of word-setting, as well as matters concerning theatre acoustics and size, music education, compositions for which instruments of the period are required, and how a style can be created (and lost).

We know that Rossini had a fine mind. What the conversations also reveal is how acute his memory was. Since the birth of modern Rossini scholarship in the late 1960s, we have come to know a vast amount about his life and times, thanks to such projects as the Fondazione Rossini's multi-volume edition of his complete letters and documents (*Gioachino Rossini: Lettere e Documenti*, Bruno Cagli and Sergio Ragni, eds. Pesaro, 1992-). There are times during his conversations with Hiller when Rossini expresses a wayward opinion: his scepticism, for example, about the truth of the story of Paganini's financial bail-out of the impoverished Berlioz. And there are occasions when he briefly dons the old familiar mask of feigned indifference about his life and career, as when he denies all knowledge of the whereabouts of his autograph manuscripts. For the most part, however, what he tells Hiller is verifiably true.

It was Rossini who invited the Hillers to join him and his wife in Trouville in September 1855. What is not known is whether the idea of a published conversation came from him or from Hiller in his capacity as a writer for Cologne's *Kölnische Zeitung*. As to Rossini's motive in allowing the conversations to be published, this may have been a simple act of kindness to Hiller, aided, perhaps, by the chance to indicate to the world that the 'Swan of Pesaro' was once again back in circulation. The other possibility concerns biography, a matter raised by Hiller during the conversations. Rossini had already been the subject of several unreliable biographies, beginning with Stendhal's semi-fictional *Vie de Rossini* published in Paris in 1824. As he moved into his seventh decade, the time was clearly ripe to begin to set the record straight.

Since Rossini and Hiller were both fluent French speakers, the conversations were largely conducted in French. Hiller had some Italian – he had spent time in Italy studying polyphony with the Palestrina scholar and administrator of the Sistine Chapel Choir Giuseppe Baini – but he would have taken Rossini's praise of his command of Italian more as a courtesy than fact.

At the end of his introduction, Hiller remarks, 'One thing of the utmost importance, which I can guarantee, is that nothing of substance has been invented by me and put into the mouth of the Maestro'. This is almost certainly true. As I know from publishing the conversations I had with the distinguished Austrian conductor Herbert von Karajan (*Conversations with Karajan*, Oxford University Press, 1989) conducting, transcribing and editing an extended series of conversations requires a certain literary legerdemain. One edits and adapts in order to purvey the substance of the conversation in a form which catches the feel of the exchanges as they actually happened. Hiller was an accomplished writer with a style which was very much of its time and place. In translating his text into modern English I have occasionally freed up the idiom without, I hope, in any way altering the substance of his and Rossini's own distinctive voice and contribution.

The conversations first appeared in German in a series of newspaper serialisations in Cologne's *Kölnische Zeitung* in October 1855 and were later reprinted by Hiller in his volume *Aus dem Tonleben unserer Zeit* (Vol.2, Leipzig, 1868, 1–84). In 1992 an Italian translation based on the Cologne texts was published in the *Bollettino del Centro Rossiniano di Studi* (Vol.XXXII, 67–132). This, however, is the first time a complete transcript has been published in English.

Trouville-sur-Mer, Normandy, 1855

By the mid-1850s the Normandy coastal town of Trouville-sur-Mer was already one of France's most exclusive resorts. The fashion for sea-bathing, which George III's visits to Weymouth on the southern English coast had done much to promote in the 1790s, finally won French royal approval in 1824 when Marie-Caroline, Duchesse de Berry set up house in the Normandy coastal down of Dieppe.

Widowed in 1820 at the age of 21 when her husband the Duc de Berry was stabbed outside the Paris Opéra by a disaffected republican saddle-maker, the duchess was the daughter-in-law of France's recently crowned Charles X. Had the 1830 July Revolution not removed the Bourbon dynasty, her son Henri would have inherited the French throne.

Rossini knew the duchess well. His wedding cantata *Le nozze di Teti, e di Peleo* had been commissioned for her marriage to the Duc de Berry in Naples in 1816. In 1825 he had created a rather grander musical pageant *Il viaggio a Reims* to mark Charles X's coronation. And in the summer of 1827 he had stayed with the duchess in her residence near Dieppe where he gave a private recital with the 19-year-old Irish baritone and composer Michael Balfe.

The arrival of the railways in the 1840s reduced the journey time from Paris to Dieppe to just four hours. More significantly, a branch line was built to Trouville-sur-Mer, a small fishing village a few miles south of Dieppe which was already much favoured by artists. It was the painter Charles Mozin (1806–62) who first put Trouville on the artistic map. (The Duchesse de Berry was a patron.) Soon many of the great names of French Impressionism were summering there. Claude Monet had a particular affection for the place.

Given Trouville's newly fashionable reputation, it comes as no

surprise that Ferdinand Hiller chose to preface the record of his conversations with Rossini with a carefully crafted prose evocation of Trouville, its topography and its people. After all, it was not only painters over whom Trouville cast its spell. Gustave Flaubert, who had family connections with the town, was one, Marcel Proust would be another.

The place where Rossini, Hiller and their wives stayed in September 1855 was Trouville's Casino-Salon, which had opened in 1847. Its architect was Desle-François Breney (1804–91), who designed much of Trouville and the neighbouring town of Deauville, transforming what had once been a pair of quiet fishing villages into resorts which by the end of the nineteenth century were closely associated with the spirit of La Belle Époque.

FERDINAND HILLER

Trouville, 1855

WHAT a beautiful September morning! There is not so much as a small cloud in the blue sky. Stirred by a fresh westerly breeze, the waves seem to take pleasure in being lightly ruffled. The charming villas by the beach and on the heights beyond lie golden in the sun. The enchanting gardens with their luxuriant flower-beds are rich in colour. Large fishing boats sway under billowing sails on the greyish waves, whilst from beneath the white houses of the harbour of Havre le Grace a black steamer moves hastily away. To the left green hills slope down to the nearby river Touques, and midway, on the unending, flat, mystical blue line over which one casts one's gaze, a sail or light cloud of smoke appears. It is a pleasing view, at once cheerful and uplifting.

Trouville has the curious character of being a cross between a fashionable beach resort and a quiet country retreat. There are entrepreneurs who would like to turn it into an important port but its fine sands will be washed and dried many times before such a thing comes to pass. A not insignificant number of distinguished French families have taken up residence here. In the fine summer months their desire is to be by the sea; in the autumn these busiest of people hunt and socialise. (In the winter, it goes without saying, life is not possible outside Paris.) The celebrated 86-year-old Chancelier Pasquier[1] comes here every year and the salon of his longstanding lady-friend Countess B. is among the most interesting in France. The wealthy families of Caen and Lisieux also consider Trouville to be their country retreat and twice a day a ferry brings over visitors from Le Havre.

There is an establishment at the baths called the Salon. A pleasantly appointed place without being in any way luxurious, it is where some

1 Étienne-Denis, duc de Pasquier (1767–1862), French statesman and member of the Académie Française. President of the Chamber of Peers 1830–48.

I

of these visitors pass their time, particularly during the afternoon and evening. French newspapers, and the occasional English one, are provided, there is a billiard room and a ballroom where twice a week members of the beau monde dance late into the night. It is possible to take lessons in dance and music here but there is no restaurant as such. One pays to enter the Salon. Since there are no gaming dens in these seaside resorts in immoral France, one has no option.[2] A covered terrace, with a beautiful view of the sea and Le Havre in the distance, runs in a semicircle around the Salon. It is here that visitors embroider, gossip, play whist and dominoes, read, smoke, perambulate and partake of other such relaxing activities. There are also in the vicinity of Trouville opportunities for those with interests in the countryside and natural history to walk or make excursions. Those in possession of a robust constitution, and an equally robust wallet, can have an excellent time here.

Among the personalities present, the one who has aroused the greatest interest is General Monet[3] who was wounded in the first assault on the Malakoff on 18 June.[4] His entire physiognomy bespeaks a personality of simple probity and modesty matched by a powerful intelligence. He spoke of the military campaign in Crimea with the greatest simplicity and sincerity: of the nature of the operation, and of the dangers and tasks undertaken and still to come.[5]

2 Only licensed casinos were permitted.

3 Monet, Count Adolphe de (1804–74). The grandson of the General Major of the armies of Augustus III of Poland, he was educated at the military academy of St-Cyr. During the Crimean War he commanded the first brigade of the French third division. He led the failed assault on the Selinghinsk redoubt on the night of 23–24 February 1855. He was shot in the hands and arm and had two fingers amputated. Edme-Adolphe Fontaine's *Attaque de la redoute de Selinghinsk par la brigade Monet* (1857, Musée National du Château et des Trianons, Versailles) shows the 50-year-old general leading the night-time charge.

4 The initial assault on the Malakoff redoubt in Sebastopol in the early hours of 18 June 1855 was bungled when the accidental firing of a French gun caused the premature launch of the attack. The redoubt finally fell, and with it Sebastopol itself, on 8 September 1855.

5 Hiller notes that the General revealed nothing which had not been reported in the newspapers. He adds that the general, whose mother was German, planned to complete his recuperation in Germany. Monet was, however, no Germanophile. Though recently retired from the French army, he fought as a reservist during the Franco-Prussian war of 1870.

However, the real lion among the guests was and remained 'the Swan of Pesaro', Gioachino Rossini. There is no doubt that for the French for the past 25 years he has been the biggest name in music, despite his absence from the country and his musical inactivity. France's so-called musical revolution is said to date from his arrival in Paris.[6] Dyed-in-the-wool royalists and red republicans unite in singing his praises.

In no country where European music is performed is there a name more *widely known* than his; nor has there yet been a more popular opera than *Il barbiere di Siviglia*. Much as we love and venerate our great German masters, not even the most confirmed Classicist would be so unjust as to fail to recognise Rossini's great genius. Any criticisms that we make – either from a national standpoint or from belief in a musical ideal – will be much weakened if we judge him against the work of his Italian predecessors and compatriots.

However, it is not the purpose of these lines to pursue such thoughts, merely to report the extraordinary attention that was afforded Rossini – a mix of awe and curiosity – and the genuine affection which was felt by those who approached him. This was a personality to win all hearts, added to which, the sufferings which poor health has obliged him to endure struck a chord with great and small alike.[7] New arrivals and passers-by would wait for the moment when they might catch sight of him. As for the residents, they spoke of nothing else. If half a day passed without his being seen, reports on his health were received with an interest equal to those of the latest dispatches from the Crimea.

6 Rossini was based in Paris between 1824 and 1838.

7 In Paris in 1843 Rossini was treated for a potentially fatal obstruction of the bladder by the acclaimed urologist Jean Civiale. Civiale had developed an early form of lithotripsy using a device inserted through the urethra with which the bladder stones were crushed. Rossini was traumatised by the treatment and the long period of isolation which followed, something which may have accelerated the onset of the depressive episodes he suffered in the late 1840s and early 1850s. Civiale's advice on the correct procedures for catheterisation did, however, enable Rossini to manage his condition. In later years, visitors to his Paris apartment were surprised to see catheters openly displayed alongside Rossini's wigs and musical instruments. The catheter, he said, was 'the best of instruments'.

This was a summer of scares about Rossini's health. The fact that he had hired a carriage and horses and taken four weeks to travel from Florence to Paris gave rise to all manner of conjecture.[8] When he then found Paris unbearable, at the very moment when all Europe was flocking there, his followers were tempted to renounce him. The simplest explanation for all this is that the noise of Paris's street traffic this summer proved insupportable for someone whose nervous system has been much weakened.

There is little wonder that a man who has been composing operas for 20 years, as well as being worshipped continuously for 45 years, now feels a touch weary. But a nabob who spends a couple of thousand pounds is still a nabob, and so the spirit of Rossini is unaltered. His wit, his memory, and his lively powers of communication all remain intact. Though two decades have passed since he composed anything, no one has the right to say that his musical genius has abated. *Guillaume Tell* was the last work he wrote.[9]

Rossini is now 63 years old. His features are little changed. It would be difficult to find a more intelligent face than his: a well-chiselled nose, an eloquent mouth, expressive eyes, and a magnificent forehead. His physiognomy is of a Southern vivacity, as eloquent in jest as it is in earnest: irresistible in expressing irony or a mood or roguishness. His voice is as pleasant as it is flexible. No South German sounds more pleasant to the ear of a well-educated North German than does Rossini. He possesses the most sociable nature imaginable. He never tires of having people around him: conversing, telling stories and — what is more commendable — listening. His is the kind of balanced personality which is found only in people of the south. He always finds the right words for children and the elderly, for nobles and persons of humbler origins, all without altering his manner. His is one of those fortunate natures in which everything is innate, where every change happens organically in and of itself. Nothing

8 Rossini left Florence in April 1855. Travelling via Nice, he arrived in Paris a month later.

9 *Guillaume Tell* was Rossini's last opera. Hiller omits to mention works such as the *Stabat mater* and the *Soirées musicales* completed in the years 1832–41.

in his art or his personality is violent, which is why he has won so many hearts.

This devotion manifests itself in all possible ways. For concerts and such events, he is always accorded the middle seat in the front row. Out on the terrace the loveliest and most elegant women gather round and pamper him. A high-ranking local dignitary from Caen earnestly sought my advice about which of the new streets in Trouville should be honoured with Rossini's name. There is also an amusing tale of a tailor, M. Cuiller, who had the honour of making a pair of trousers for Rossini. When he delivered the trousers, he asked somewhat bashfully if he could add to his shop sign the legend, 'Tailor to M. Rossini'. Rossini protested that he looked like a butter-seller. 'You'll lose your reputation if you do that.' But the tailor was not to be deterred. He persisted. The Maestro laughed. And today on the main street of Trouville visitors may see a sign that reads:

Cuiller
Tailor to Mr G. Rossini

I had been introduced to Rossini when I was a young man in Paris. Later I often saw him in Italy where he was always attentive and agreeable to the highest degree. During my two or three weeks in Trouville I spent the majority of my time in his company. We walked for hours up and down on the small terrace overlooking the sea. We would occasionally stop our ramble to play a game of dominoes but the conversation continued even then, despite the fact that the games were played extremely seriously.

Rossini was inexhaustible in providing me with information. He was also insatiable in his requests for news of people and events on which I could inform him. The lack of a good instrument meant that I played for him only occasionally but music and musicians were our main topic of conversation. As I have already mentioned, Rossini's memory is extraordinarily retentive. His knowledge of differing works and composers is far larger than most German musicians would suspect. As to his judgment, it struck me as being sharp, penetrating and impartial. He knows everything about everything and does everything justice. It is natural that in a career such as his he has seen, heard and experienced much that was endlessly interesting. It is my hope that, by committing to paper whilst they remain fresh in the memory those Rossini stories which were particularly interesting or amusing, I can do a service to many artists and friends of music.

As to my including myself in the narrative – as little as possible, I should add – I hope I may be forgiven for this. The conversations follow no preordained plan as laid down by the Maestro. One word led to another and, so (to avoid the whole thing ending up as a shapeless mess) I have allowed the informal and aphoristic give-and-take of our conversation to follow its original path.

One thing of the utmost importance, which I can guarantee, is that nothing of substance has been invented by me and put into the mouth of the Maestro.

G. ROSSINI.

Conversations with Rossini

1

ROSSINI: These journalists! Shortly before I left Paris someone wrote that I disliked railway travel almost as much as I dislike German music! What do you make of that?

HILLER: If it was true, Maestro, you would make many journeys by rail.

ROSSINI: I not only love the great musicians of Germany, in my youth they had pride of place in my studies. Since when I have neglected no opportunity to know them better. What joy I experienced playing the works of Bach!

HILLER: I have never enjoyed his marvellous keyboard pieces more than when playing them for you.

ROSSINI: What a colossus Bach is! To write such a *quantity* of compositions and in *such* a style! It is incredible. At what stage is that beautiful edition of his works? I first heard of it from a Leipzig family who visited me in Florence. After that I received two volumes but I would like to have others.[10]

HILLER: Nothing is easier. You must take out a subscription.

ROSSINI: With the greatest pleasure!

HILLER: It would a source of great pride to me to have your name among the subscribers.

ROSSINI: The portrait of Bach in the first volume is magnificent; it expresses an extraordinary spiritual power. He must also have been a renowned virtuoso.

10 *J.S. Bach: Werke*, ed. Bach-Gesellschaft, i-xlvii (Leipzig, 1851–99). At the time of Rossini's meeting with Hiller, five volumes had been published: three volumes of church cantatas, the *St Matthew Passion* and a volume of keyboard pieces including the *Goldberg Variations*. By the time of Rossini's death in 1868, 16 of the 47 volumes had been published.

HILLER: The most important composers of our time are happy if they can learn to play one of his pieces well with his improvisatory spirit.

ROSSINI: Men such as him are rare. Are many of his works performed in Germany?'

HILLER: Some, but not as many as should be.

ROSSINI: Unfortunately it is not possible in Italy – now less than ever. We cannot assemble the large amateur choirs you have in Germany. At one time we had good voices in churches and chapels but that's all gone. After Baini's death even the Sistine Chapel choir is in decline.[11] And speaking of that, where are we with the controversy concerning the authenticity of Mozart's *Requiem*? Are we any nearer a reliable conclusion?[12]

HILLER: Nothing that you don't already know.

ROSSINI: The 'Confutatis' at least cannot be denied to Mozart. [*Rossini sings the opening.*] It is superb! And the *sotto voce* end! Those modulations! I have always had a fondness for the use of *sotto voce* as a choral device but every time I hear that it sends shivers down my spine. Poor Mozart!

HILLER: I've seen it written that Mozart laughed barely more than three times during his life. What do you say to such nonsense? There are many things I need to know about. For example, is it true that after a brief while you asked your elderly teacher Padre Mattei if you knew sufficient to write an opera – and when the answer was yes you were up and away?

ROSSINI: Nothing could be further from the truth! I studied three years at the Liceo in Bologna. During that time I needed to do everything possible to ensure that I could support both myself and my parents. I managed, though I have to admit it

---

11 Baini, Giuseppe (1775–1844). Italian musicologist, Palestrina scholar, composer and administrator. Baini joined the choir of the papal chapel in 1795. In 1814 he was entrusted with the reorganisation of the chapel's archives and in 1819 became its general administrator.

12 The authenticity of parts of Mozart's *Requiem* had first been questioned by the musicologist Gottfried Weber in 1825.

was in pretty poor measure. Theatres paid me six paoli a night to accompany recitatives on the harpsichord.[13] I also had a beautiful voice, so I could sing in churches. In addition to that Mattei made me write exercises of a non-ecclesiastical nature – pieces which a singer like Zamboni could insert into an opera or a recital, for which I was also paid a pittance.[14] Once I had worked my way through counterpoint and fugue, I asked Mattei what I should do next. 'Plainchant and canon' came the reply. 'And how long must I devote to that?' 'About two years.' I explained to the good father that I couldn't wait that long. He was always well disposed towards me, so he understood. In later years I often had cause to regret that I didn't work longer with him.

HILLER: So you were able to do without canon! I would imagine that Mattei was a very capable teacher.

ROSSINI: With a pen in his hand, he was superb. His corrections were highly instructive. But he was extremely taciturn. Spoken explanations had to be dragged out of him more or less by force. Have you seen any of his compositions?

HILLER: I've never come across his work.

ROSSINI: If you return to Bologna, you must not fail to visit our Liceo. The compositions are exclusively of church music. The solo writing is not so good but the writing for full choir is splendid.

HILLER: I must return to your youth, dear Maestro. You had already composed a number of things before beginning your studies?

ROSSINI: There is an entire opera, *Demetrio e Polibio*, which is always mentioned later in my list of works.[15] The music was

13 About £3.50.

14 Zamboni, Luigi (1767–1837), Italian *basso buffo*. A native of Bologna, he created the role of Figaro in Rossini's *Il barbiere di Siviglia* (Rome, 1816).

15 The opera was written around the time of Rossini's 18th birthday.

originally written for the Mombelli family, though at the time we didn't know that it would end up as an opera. During my first month of work with Mattei I couldn't finish anything. I trembled over every bass note. Every middle voice gave me a small shudder of terror. Only later did I regain my former courage.

HILLER: That was fortunate. So you had already begun to learn music in Pesaro?

ROSSINI: I left Pesaro in early childhood. My father was the town trumpeter and also played the horn in the opera house. All went reasonably well until the French arrived.[16] My mother, who had a beautiful voice, helped us out during the emergency and so we left Pesaro. Poor mother! She was not without talent despite the fact that she couldn't read music. She sang *orecchiante*, as we say, by ear. Incidentally, 80 per cent of Italian singers do the same.

HILLER: I cannot believe it![17]

ROSSINI: It's absolutely true. To learn to sing an aria by ear: this can be done. But how these people learn the inner part of an ensemble has always been a bit of a mystery to me.

HILLER: So where did you begin your musical studies?

ROSSINI: In Bologna.

HILLER: And who was that with?

ROSSINI: A teacher called Prinetti from Novara. He gave me lessons on the spinet. He was a strange fellow. He manufactured liquor and gave music lessons to make ends meet.[18] He never owned a bed. He slept standing up.

HILLER: Standing up! You're joking, Maestro.

16 5 February, 1797. However, it was the return of Austrian forces two years later that caused the family real difficulties. An outspoken republican, Rossini's father was briefly imprisoned.

17 Singers who learned by ear could be found in Italian opera houses as late as the 1960s.

18 Giuseppe Prinetti did have some other sources of income. He was a keyboard player at the Teatro Comunale, Bologna and also composed.

ROSSINI: It's as I say. He slept, well wrapped up in his cloak, propped up against a corner of the arcade. The night-watchmen knew him, so they left him alone. He would turn up early, drag me from my bed – something I didn't relish – and make me play. Sometimes he wasn't sufficiently rested, so he slept whilst I played, still standing up. I occasionally took advantage of this by slipping back into bed. When he woke and found me in bed I calmed him down by assuring him while he slept I had played the piece through without mistakes. His method was not exactly up-to-date. For example, I was playing scales with thumb and forefinger.

HILLER: That would have been as damaging as your neglect of canon! But who were your other early teachers?

ROSSINI: A certain Angelo Tesei taught me figured bass, accompaniment and *solfeggio*. My advanced singing lessons were with an important tenor of the time, a man called Babini.[19]

HILLER: You had a charming voice, I'm told?

ROSSINI: As a boy I sang beautifully. It was at that time that I appeared on stage in the role of a child in Paer's *Camilla*.[20] But that was all.

HILLER: Did any of your contemporaries at the Liceo achieve fame?

ROSSINI: In my first year there, Morlacchi[21] was in his final year. And my third year was Donizetti's[22] first.

19 Babini, Matteo (1754–1816), Italian tenor. After a distinguished international career, he took leave of the stage in Bologna in 1802.

20 Paer, Ferdinando (1771–1839), Italian composer and a central figure in the development of *opera semiseria* during the first decade of the nineteenth century.

21 Morlacchi, Francesco (1784–1841), Italian composer, later based in Dresden. His *Il barbiere di Siviglia*, a decidedly old-fashioned affair, heavily indebted to Paisiello's setting of 1782, had its premiere in Dresden in April 1816, two months after the opening in Rome of Rossini's radical new treatment of Beaumarchais's prose comedy.

22 Donizetti, Gaetano (1797–1848), Italian composer, close follower of Rossini and, with Bellini, his most important immediate successor. Rossini championed his music in Paris in the 1830s. Donizetti conducted the first Italian performance of Rossini's *Stabat mater* in Bologna in 1842.

HILLER: Was not Donizetti a Simone Mayr pupil?[23]

ROSSINI: He carried out a number of experiments with Mayr but his real musical training was in Bologna.

HILLER: You must tell me more about your early years. My interest in this is not easily satisfied!

ROSSINI: Another time, my dear Ferdinand. Here comes my wife[24] – it is lunchtime. After lunch we shall smoke a cigar together!

23 Mayr, Simone (1763–1845), German composer and writer who was a leading figure in the development of *opera seria* between the mid-1790s to the early 1820s.

24 Pélissier, Olympe (1797–1878), Rossini's second wife whom he married in 1846 after the death of his first wife, Isabella Colbran-Rossini. Courtesan, mistress of the painter Vernet, and model for Fedora in Balzac's *La Peau de chagrin*, Olympe became Rossini's close companion in Paris in the early 1830s. She moved to Bologna in 1837 and was responsible for Rossini's return to Paris in the year of these conversations, 1855. Her care for Rossini during his physical and depressive illnesses of the 1840s and early 1850s, and her exceptional skills as a society hostess, helped sustain him through the last three decades of his life. Without her remarkable care, his return to composition in the years 1857–68 might not have come about.

2

When we resumed that evening, I asked Rossini about the Mombelli family for which he wrote Demetrio e Polibio. *It is not often that one meets a family that requires an opera to be written.*

ROSSINI: Mombelli was a first-rate tenor who had two daughters. One sang soprano, the other alto. They also recruited a bass, so that without further help they had a vocal quartet which was able to perform in Bologna, Milan and other towns which staged operas.[25] That's how they started in Bologna with a work by Portogallo, small but utterly charming.

HILLER: A Portuguese composer?[26]

ROSSINI: An Italian, in effect. He was not without talent. His writing for the voice was particularly fine, so his works were favoured by a number of prominent singers. My first wife Mme Colbran[27] had some 40 of pieces by him in her repertory. The way I made Mombelli's acquaintance was rather curious. And since you like my stories, I shall tell you.

HILLER: Tell away, Maestro!

25 The quartet consisted of Domenico Mombelli (tenor), Ester Mombelli (soprano), Marianna Mombelli (contralto) and Lodovico Olivieri (bass). Ester Mombelli became a noted Rossini interpreter. She made her Paris debut in 1824 singing the title role in *La Cenerentola* at the Théâtre des Italiens.

26 Portugal, Marcos António [Marc'Antonio Portogallo] (1762–1830), Portuguese-born composer and conductor. Born and trained in Lisbon, he first visited Italy in 1787. Between 1792 and 1800, he wrote 21 Italian operas, both *seria* and *buffa*. In 1811 he joined the Portuguese court in exile in Rio de Janeiro where he died in 1830.

27 Colbran, Isabella (1785–1845), Spanish soprano and Rossini's first wife. She studied in Madrid and in Paris with the celebrated castrato Crescentini. In 1806 she moved to Bologna, where Rossini first heard her, and in 1811 to Naples where she established herself as *prima donna assoluta* of the San Carlo company. During his Naples years (1815–22) Rossini created a succession of dramatically powerful roles for her. She retired from the stage in 1824, two years after her marriage to Rossini. The marriage was dissolved in 1837.

ROSSINI: At the age of 13, I was already an admirer of the fair
sex. One of my friends or, shall I say, protectoresses wanted
an aria from an opera which the Mombellis were staging. I
went to the copyist but he refused to give it me. So I approached
Mombelli who also refused me. 'Not that it makes the slightest
difference,' I told him. 'Tonight I shall hear the piece one
more time and then write it out.' 'We'll see about that,' said
Mombelli. I listened to the piece again with close attention,
made a piano reduction, and took it to Mombelli. He didn't
want to believe me. He screamed about being betrayed by the
copyist and other such things. 'If you don't trust me,' I said,
'then I will listen twice more to the opera, write out the entire
score and lay it before your eyes.' My great – and in this case
entirely justified – confidence in myself overcame his distrust,
and we became good friends.

HILLER: I have often had occasion to convince myself of your
extraordinary musical memory. But to commit an entire opera
to paper is truly amazing

ROSSINI: It wasn't *Le nozze di Figaro*! Still, I'm happy to boast
about the strength of my musical memory in those years.

HILLER: It is a special talent! I have known great musicians
who did not know by heart compositions of their own which
they had played a hundred times. Others, by contrast, had
entire libraries in their head. Mendelssohn came into this
category. He once accompanied an entire Bach Passion from
memory.

ROSSINI: Haydn oratorios were something I could attempt
from a young age – *The Creation* in particular. I knew even the
smallest recitative by heart. That said, I had accompanied it
and played it through quite often.

HILLER: But I must return to *Demetrio e Polibio*. As you
will realise, I have an archaeologist's instincts! So Mombelli
engaged you to write this opera?

ROSSINI: He gave me words for a duet and then words for an aria. For each piece he paid me two piastre, which was a great spur to industry.[28] So that's how, without knowing it, I came to make my first opera. I had some good advice from my singing teacher Babini.[29] He was passionately opposed to certain melodic figures which were fashionable at the time and used all his eloquence to make me avoid them.

HILLER: When I was in Italy a quartet drawn from *Demetrio e Polibio* still enjoyed a certain notoriety as evidence of your youthful precocity. Was anything more done to the opera when it finally came to the stage?

ROSSINI: I wasn't even there. Mombelli put it on in Milan without my knowledge.[30] What surprised most people about the quartet was that it ended not with a normal cadence but with a form of vocal exclamation. As for the duet, which has been much performed, the main thing about that is that it's very simple.

HILLER: You grew up singing and performing, and you had a fine voice, so is it not strange that you never thought of becoming an opera singer?

ROSSINI: I had no other thought, my dear. But, you see, I wanted to learn my craft more thoroughly than that of most of the singers I came across at the time. Things came easily to me. I soon mastered the harpsichord. In the meantime my voice changed and I found my compositions were being favourably received. In that sense it was almost by accident that I ended up as a composer – though I was aware from the outset that the fees paid to singers were out of all proportion to those we composers received!

28 About £12 an item.
29 See n.19.
30 The first performance was at Rome's Teatro Valle on 18 May, 1812. All the music is by Rossini, with the exception of nos 12–15 in Act 2.

HILLER: Heaven knows, Beethoven barely earned as much in his entire career as Cruvelli earns in a single year at the Paris Opéra.[31]

ROSSINI: Certainly it wasn't as crazy as it is now, but things were similar. If the composer earned 50 ducats, the singer received 1000. I confess I have never been able to get over this injustice, and have often expressed my discontent on the matter. 'You're incompetent,' I tell them. 'You are no better at singing than I am, yet you earn in one evening more than I am paid for an entire score!' But what's the point! The German composers aren't rich either!

HILLER: Definitely not, Maestro! But they get employment which, even if the pay is not great, provides enough for their immediate needs. No German composer could live of the proceeds of his operas. In Italy, however, it seems that nowadays the situation is better.

ROSSINI: Incomparably so. Goodness knows how many Italian opera composers lived at subsistence level in the old days. For me, working for Barbaja wasn't much different.[32]

HILLER: *Tancredi* was your first hugely successful opera.[33] How much did it make?

ROSSINI: 500 francs.[34] And in Venice when I wrote *Semiramide*, my final opera for Italy, they paid me 5000 francs,[35]

31 Cruvelli, Sophie [Crüwell] (1826–1907), German soprano. In 1855 she created the role of La Duchesse Hélène in Verdi's *Les Vêpres Siciliennes* at the Paris Opéra. She retired the following year.

32 Barbaja, Domenico (1778–1841), Italian impresario. The most astute and characterful impresario of his era, Barbaja ran the royal theatres in Naples during the years 1809-24, 1827-31 and 1836-40. Rossini worked for him between 1815 and 1822. Though Rossini was handsomely rewarded, he complained that Barbaja would have had him washing the dishes if he could have got away with it.

33 *Tancredi*, Teatro La Fenice, Venice, 6 February, 1813. It was 'Di tanti palpiti', the *cabaletta* to *Tancredi's* Act 1 *cavatina*, which won popularity across Europe.

34 £1800.

35 £18000. *Semiramide*, Venice, 1823.

which the management and wider public considered to be a form of highway robbery.

HILLER: You have the consolation that the singers, the impresarios and the music publishers became rich as a result of your efforts.

ROSSINI: A nice consolation! Apart from my stay in England, I never earned enough from my compositions to set aside savings. And the money I made in London was as an accompanist rather than as a composer.[36]

HILLER: But this was because you were a famous composer!

ROSSINI: My friends advised me about this. It may have been prejudice, but I had an aversion to being paid to provide piano accompaniments. In London I set that aside. All they really wanted was to see my nose and listen to my wife. For our participation in a musical evening I charged a fairly high fee of £50.[37] We did about 60 such engagements and it was well worth the effort. In London musicians do anything to make money. I experienced the most wonderful things there.

HILLER: In such places it's difficult to trust one's eyes, let alone one's ears.

ROSSINI: For the first soirée I attended, it was said that Puzzi, the famous horn-player,[38] would be present, and Dragonetti, the even more famous double-bass.[39] I thought they would both be playing solos but nothing of the sort! They were there to help me accompany. 'So do you have the music for all these pieces?' I asked. 'God forbid!' was the answer. 'But we get

---

36 Rossini and his first wife spent seven months in England in 1823-24.

37 £5000.

38 Puzzi, Giovanni (1792-1876), Italian horn virtuoso who moved to London in 1815.

39 Dragonetti, Domenico (1763-1846), celebrated Italian-born but mainly London-based double bass player. He played with Haydn and Beethoven and was revered by fellow virtuosi such as Paganini and Liszt. During his stay in London, Rossini was commissioned by the banker and amateur cellist Philip Salomons to write a *Duetto* for cello and double-bass for Salomons and Dragonetti. Rediscovered in 1968, the work has been recorded.

well paid and will accompany as we think best.' I found these improvised accompaniments a bit too hazardous, so I asked Dragonetti to confine himself to a few pizzicati whenever I winked at him. As for Puzzi, I asked him to reinforce the cadence with a few notes, which as a good musician he could do with ease. So there were no mishaps and everyone was happy.

HILLER: Priceless! But the English, I gather, have made great progress in the field of music. In London today there is a lot of good music, well performed and listened to with attention – at least, in public concerts. It's a rather more depressing story where private salons are concerned, with talentless people having the effrontery to give lessons in disciplines they know nothing about.

ROSSINI: In London I met an incompetent part-time flautist, a certain X., who had made a fortune as a teacher of piano and singing. There was also an incredibly sought-after singing teacher who couldn't even read music. He would take along an accompanist who would mug up the piece beforehand. Still, he had a beautiful voice.

HILLER: So are you of the opinion, Maestro, that the really good singing teacher is something of a miracle, in as much as he has the doubly difficult task of creating the very instrument with which he makes music?

ROSSINI: The majority of great singers of our time – Rubini, Pasta and others – owe more to their own talents than to their teachers. The true art of *bel canto* ended with the castrati. That much must be conceded, for all that we should not wish for their return. Their art was everything to them, which is why they devoted themselves to their training with the greatest diligence and care. They invariably became capable musicians, which meant that if something went amiss with the voice, they at least remained excellent teachers.

HILLER: Who would you consider to be the best singing teachers at the moment?

ROSSINI: I have tremendous respect for Pier Marini in Paris.[40] In Florence, Lamperti can do wonderful work preparing non-beginners for the stage.[41] Is there a good voice teacher in your conservatory in Cologne?

HILLER: Reinthaler knows his stuff, as few in Germany do and what's more he is an excellent composer.[42] But I have a proposal to make, Maestro.

ROSSINI: And that would be?

HILLER: If you would take a singing class in our conservatory, I could offer you a fee of 300 Thaler as well as free accommodation. Is that not tempting?[43]

ROSSINI: Very much so, my dear Ferdinand. We shall discuss the details later.

40 Unidentified. Hiller may have misheard the name. The most celebrated singing teacher in Europe at the time was Manuel García the younger (1805–1906).

41 Lamperti, Francesco (1813–92), Italian singing teacher. By 1855 he was teaching in Milan not Florence. Two of his pupils, Emma Albani (1847–1930) and Charles Santley (1834–1922), recorded for the gramophone.

42 Reinthaler, Karl (1822–96), German composer and conductor. One of his teachers was the tenor Giulio Bordogni (1789–1856) who created the role of Libenskof in Rossini's *Il viaggio a Reims* in Paris in 1825.

43 It is not clear what the proposed fee – in the region of £2500 at today's prices – would have involved. In the event, Rossini did not take up the offer.

3

Rossini sang the beginning of a string quartet by Haydn.

ROSSINI: Can a piece begin in a nobler manner? What momentum! And such elegance in the theme!

HILLER: To my mind Haydn's string quartets have been surpassed by no composer, not even by Beethoven himself.

ROSSINI: Enchanting works. How lovingly the instruments interact! And the subtlety of the modulations! All great composers make beautiful transitions but for me Haydn's have always had a special charm.

HILLER: Were you able to hear the quartets in Italy?

ROSSINI: This began in Bologna in my youth. I formed a string quartet in which I played the viola to the best of my abilities. When we began, the first violin knew only a few pieces by Haydn but I was always at him, urging him on, so in the end we knew quite a few. As a student I had a particular love of Haydn. I directed *The Creation* at the Liceo in Bologna. I had the entire score from memory, which meant that the performers couldn't get away with a thing. I also studied *The Seasons* when I became director of Bologna's philharmonic concerts after leaving the Liceo.

HILLER: *The Seasons* is perhaps even richer in invention than *The Creation*. The text allows for a greater diversity.

ROSSINI: Perhaps so. But *The Creation* concerns higher things and that, for me, gives it the greater appeal. How beautiful this aria is [*Rossini sings*]. And the chorus in B flat and Raphael's aria. And what a wonderful instrumental movement we have in Haydn's depiction of Chaos! Nothing sticks deeper than the impressions one receives in one's earliest youth. In Vienna I met a well-known Italian by the name of Carpani who had often visited Haydn in his home.⁴⁴ He never tired of speaking of the master's goodness of heart, his gentleness and modesty. Haydn was also, in the highest degree, fairminded towards others. He told Mozart's father, in the simplest language, that he considered his son to be the greatest of all composers. That certainly was his view, and he was right!

HILLER: I have a different feeling about Haydn's operas. It's curious but they don't seem to be as great.

ROSSINI: I was able to look through them in Vienna with a passionate admirer of Haydn who claimed to know the entire œuvre.⁴⁵ They are minor works with occasional reminders of the great composer. I imagine Haydn composed them as a favour to Prince Esterhazy and his singers. Do you know his cantata *Arianna*?⁴⁶

HILLER: I played it through many years ago but I've never heard it – and, to my shame, I remember little about it.

ROSSINI: The oratorios aside, it is the vocal work by Haydn which is most dear to me – the *Adagio* in particular is very beautiful. [*Rossini sings.*]⁴⁷

HILLER: You know our German master better than I do. I am beginning to envy you! Do you know your Italian predecessors as well?

ROSSINI: I have read through much of the music.

HILLER: Have you seen many of Paisiello's opera?

ROSSINI: When I was young, Paisiello had more or less

44 Carpani, Giuseppe (1752–1825), Italian poet, librettist and critic. His *Le Haydine, ovvero Lettere sulla vita e le opere del celebre Maestro Giuseppe Haydn* (Milan, 1812, 2/1823) was widely admired, not least by Stendhal who published his own plagiarised version. Carpani accompanied Rossini when he visited Beethoven in Vienna in 1822.

45 Carpani, presumably.

46 *Arianna a Naxos*, Hob. XXVIb:2, [mezzo] soprano, hpd/pf, 14 March, 1790.

47 The aria Rossini refers to begins with a phrase which recalls the Countess's 'Dove sono?' from Mozart's *Le nozze di Figaro*, which Haydn was thinking of staging at the time.

disappeared from the Italian stage.[48] Generali, Fioravanti, Paer and, above all, Simone Mayr were the order of the day.

HILLER: Do you love Paisiello?

ROSSINI: His music is pleasant to the ear without being remarkable either harmonically or melodically, so I had no great interest in it. His principle was to build an entire movement out a single small motif – which made for little life and even less dramatic expression.

HILLER: You knew him personally?

ROSSINI: I saw him at Naples after his return from Paris, where he had made a fortune. Napoleon liked his music, which Paisiello boasted about in a somewhat naïve way. He wanted everyone to know that the great emperor was an admirer of his music, not least because he could 'listen to it whilst thinking of other things'. Strange praise! In Paisiello's time it was the *gentleness* of his music that was generally appreciated. Every age has its particular taste.

HILLER: Was Paisiello an interesting person?

ROSSINI: He was handsome, strong and very imposing. But he was hideously uncultured and insignificant beyond measure. You should read his letters! I'm not talking about his handwriting or spelling. Put that aside. It's the dullness of expression and shallowness of thought that are so unbelievable! Cimarosa was entirely different.[49] There was a fine, cultivated mind. Do you know any of his works?

HILLER: *Il matrimonio segreto*, of course. And I've also seen *Gli Orazi*.[50]

---

48 Paisiello, Giovanni (1740–1816), Italian composer. Paisiello's most celebrated opera *Il barbiere di Siviglia* (St Petersburg, 1782) was still extant in Rossini's time: so much so that, at its first performance in Rome in February 1816, Rossini's setting of Beaumarchais's play was entitled *Almaviva*. Rossini changed the title shortly after Paisiello's death in June 1816.

49 Cimaroso, Domenico (1749–1801), Italian composer.

50 *Gli Orazi ed i Curiazi* (Venice, 1796). Cimarosa's republican sympathies, which would lead to his imprisonment in Naples in 1799, are evident in the opera.

ROSSINI: *Gli Orazi* is not so good but there's a comic opera *Le trame deluse* which is splendid.[51]

HILLER: Better than *Il matrimonio segreto?*

ROSSINI: Infinitely more important. There is a finale to the second act – it is almost too big for a *finale ultimo* – which is a true masterpiece. Unfortunately the libretto is pitifully bad. I also remember an aria from his oratorio *Isaaco* which contains a harmonic shift that is astoundingly dramatic.[52] Pure inspiration – because, as you know, he was not for the most part a great harmonist.

HILLER: It is difficult for us non-Italians to get access to these works. To do this even once, you need to spend an entire year in Italy. The library of the Naples Conservatoire must contain the most extraordinary treasures.

ROSSINI: It's incredible what has been accumulated. They have a complete set of Cimarosa manuscripts which once belonged to Cardinal Consalvi.[53] He had a real passion for Cimarosa. Nothing gave him greater pleasure than to have one of his favourite's pieces sung for him. I did so often during my time in Rome. He was deeply grateful for that.

HILLER: And your own manuscripts, Maestro, I don't believe you possess many.

ROSSINI: Not a note.

HILLER: But where on earth are they?

ROSSINI: Heaven knows. I had the right to request them back from the copyists after a year, but I've never used it. Some

---

51 *Le trame deluse* (Naples, 1786). The title means 'Tricks Discovered'. A vital, witty, neatly written *Commedia per musica*, it contains some fine 'patter' writing for the *basso buffo*.

52 Rossini is referring to Cimarosa's *Il sacrifizio d'Abramo* (Naples, 1786).

53 Consalvi, Ercole (1757–1824), cardinal and diplomat. He was Cardinal Secretary of State to Pius VII from 1814 to 1823. In addition to being an admirer and collector of the works of Cimarosa, he took a close interest in the musical life of the papal states.

may be in Naples, others are in Paris. Their fate remains unknown to me.[54]

HILLER: Have you not preserved the things you wrote during your studies with Padre Mattei?

ROSSINI: I kept them for quite a while but one day, when I returned to Bologna, they were nowhere to be found. Whether they had been thrown away or stolen, or sold as waste paper, I've no idea.

HILLER: You'll be telling me, Maestro, that you don't even have any published editions or piano reductions of your operas!

ROSSINI: What use would they be? It is years since I made music in my home.

HILLER: And what of the opera *Ermione* which one of your biographers says is being secretly preserved to be handed down to posterity?[55]

ROSSINI: It's with the rest.

HILLER: You told me previously that it was too dramatic, and that it was a fiasco.

ROSSINI: And rightly so. It was very boring!

HILLER: So you are saying that there was no aria, no end-of-act finale, nothing that could send the audience into raptures?

ROSSINI: You're very kind. But there was nothing. It was all recitative and declamation. There's a *cavatina* I wrote for

54 Rossini is not being entirely truthful. The manuscripts of eight of the nine *opere serie* he wrote for Naples in 1815–22 remained in his possession. (The ninth had stayed in Naples.) The whereabouts of other manuscripts, including that of *Il barbiere di Siviglia*, may have been known to him, though he no longer owned them. It is true that none of the five *farse* he wrote for Venice between 1810 and 1813 remained in his possession, though in the late 1850s two of the manuscripts – *L'occasione fa il ladro* and *Il signor Bruschino* – were brought to him for authentication by private collectors. The manuscripts of all but three of Rossini's 39 operas have survived. The majority are in the Fondazione Rossini in Pesaro, the institute and conservatory set up under the terms of Rossini's will to administer his legacy.

55 Based on Racine's tragedy *Andromaque*, the opera had its *prima* in Naples on 27 March 1819. It was coolly received and ran for just five performances. Though Rossini later made use of some of its music, he became less and less inclined to press for its revival. His evasion of Hiller's questioning disguises the real hurt he felt at the work's rejection. He had told

David – the poor fellow had to have something to sing.[56] It's done the rounds so you probably know it. [*Rossini sings the principal theme.*]

HILLER: I've heard it many times but had no idea it came from this opera. But here comes General Monet. We must ask him about the latest telegraphic dispatches.

ROSSINI: We must do that. Strange music is being performed here, robustly orchestrated! When will we reach the finale?

---

the Escudier brothers in Paris in the 1840s, '*Ermione* is my little *Guillaume Tell* and it will not see the light of day until my death'. Just how wrong contemporary reaction to the piece had been was confirmed when the opera enjoyed a triumphant revival at the 1987 Pesaro Festival.

56 David, Giovanni (1790-1864), Italian tenor noted for the brilliance and beauty of his singing in high-lying roles. Two years after singing the role of Don Narciso in *Il turco in Italia* in Milan in 1814, he joined Rossini in Naples where he created the roles of Rodrigo in *Otello*, Ricciardo in *Ricciardo e Zoraide*, Oreste in *Ermione*, Giacomo V in *La donna del lago* and Ilo in *Zelmira*. As Hiller's remark confirms, the *cavatina* 'Che sorda al mesto pianto' held a regular place in the recital repertory throughout the nineteenth century.

4

Our esteemed Master Neukomm was in Trouville for two weeks in September visiting friends.[57] *It was 25 years since he and Rossini had met and since Rossini wished to see him I went along too. Rossini suddenly remembered that Neukomm had once been instructed by the Duchess of Vaudemont*[58] *to build an Aeolian harp for her and that he carried out the work on the estate of his friend Aguado.*[59] *Those two fine people were well matched to one another. I had told Rossini a lot about Neukomm, in particular the unbelievable and truly admirable things that had him tied to his desk from first thing in the morning. And it was with this that Rossini began.*

ROSSINI: You are still working tirelessly, Signor Cavaliere.

NEUKOMM: When I can no longer work put me between six boards and nail them together, because I will no longer wish to continue living.

ROSSINI: You have the same passion for hard work that I have for idleness!

NEUKOMM: The 40 operas that you have written do not exactly bear that out.

ROSSINI: That's all a long time ago. And you need to know, too, that it was a nerve-racking business. But let's leave that.

---

57 Neukomm, Sigismund von (1778–1858), Salzburg-born composer, pianist and scholar. A pupil and friend of Joseph Haydn, he settled in Paris in 1809. His friendship with the French politician and diplomat Talleyrand brought him to international notice during the Congress of Vienna, 1814–15, for which Neukomm wrote a Requiem in C minor in memory of King Louis XVI. Between 1816 and 1821 he worked at the court of John VI of Portugal in Rio de Janeiro. Returning to Paris, he became one of the most well connected and widely travelled figures of his age. His vast output of predominantly choral music is now largely forgotten.

58 Princesse de Vaudémont (1763–1833). Married in 1778 to the Prince de Vaudémont and widowed in 1812, she was an influential figure in Bourbon circles.

59 Aguado, Alejandro Maria (1785–1842), Spanish-born banker and from 1827 patron, friend and financial adviser to Rossini.

You have travelled extensively and even spent many years in Brazil?

NEUKOMM: I accepted the post of court Kapellmeister as the teacher of the young Prince Pedro who had a real love of music.[60] He even devoted himself to composition.

ROSSINI: He was kind enough to send me a decoration.[61] Later when he arrived in Paris somewhat against his will, I thanked him for this. Since I had heard about his compositions, I proposed that we should perform some of them at the Théâtre Italien, a proposal he gladly accepted.

NEUKOMM: He would have conducted them himself if you had asked him!

ROSSINI: Not possible! He sent me a *cavatina* which I wrote out with an added blast of trombone tone. It had a good performance at the Théâtre Italien and was well enough received. Dom Pedro looked very happy sitting in his box. Anyway, he thanked me most warmly afterwards.

HILLER: I remember the Countess B telling me how Dom Pedro arrived at the Tuileries that evening completely transfigured. He claimed it had been the happiest experience of his entire life. The countess said that, for a man who had just lost an empire, such demonstrations of enthusiasm seemed a little strange. I suggested to her that it is not necessarily the most important things in life which give us the greatest pleasure.

---

60 Pedro de Alcântara (1798–1834), later King Pedro I of Brazil and, briefly, king of Portugal. In 1831 he abdicated in favour of his son Pedro II and sailed for Europe. He died of tuberculosis in September 1834 only months after defeating forces fighting for the return of Portugal's absolutist regime.
61 Knight of the Order of the Southern Cross.

One morning we visited Neukomm at home. He had a small har-
monium in his room to which he had made a number of adjustments
and improvements. Full of youthful vivacity (he was 77 at the
time) he explained all the details and asked Rossini if he would like
to try the instrument. Rossini sat down and played as well as he
could a couple of dozen bars of 'Chaos' from The Creation *which*
of course moved Haydn's old pupil deeply. Then Neukomm and I
played a movement from Haydn's Seven Last Words *which*
Neukomm had transcribed for piano and harmonium. We learned
that he had made similar transcriptions of the most important works
of Handel, Haydn and Mozart – simply for his own pleasure and
that of his friends. Rossini was visibly touched. When we left he
said, 'This dedication, this true and simple love of the arts, is wor-
thy of the greatest admiration. There is no economic interest at
stake and no vanity, at least none to speak of. For that I have the
greatest respect!'

5

HILLER: Did your extraordinary success not go to your head? Given how young you were at the time, there would be no surprise if it had.

ROSSINI: My extraordinary success! But to be serious about this, I have always been as unperturbed by a success as I have been by a fiasco. All of which I owe to an experience in my youth which I have never forgotten.

HILLER: What was that?

ROSSINI: Even before I wrote my first opera, I saw in Venice the first performance of a *farsa* by Simone Mayr. You must remember that Mayr was very much the hero of the hour. As many as 20 of his operas had met with huge success in Venice. Despite this, the audience that evening treated him as if he was a jumped-up ignoramus. It's not possible to conceive such cruelty. This really shocked me. 'Is this how you reward a man who has brought such joy over so many years?' I asked. 'Can you take such a liberty merely because you have paid a couple of paoli entrance fee? If so, it's certainly not worth taking your opinion to heart.' And that, to the best of my ability, is how I have dealt with such matters.

HILLER: You yourself were not always let off lightly!

ROSSINI: I'd say! You know what happened on the first night of *Il barbiere*.[62] And that was not the only occasion. There was one evening, however, when I was really touched by the Venetians. It was the first night of *Sigismondo* and they were bored rigid. I could see how eager they were to vent their

---

62 The performance took place in a near-riot brought about, in part, by the presence of a pro-Paisiello claque in the house. The Rosina, Gertrude Righetti Giorgi, later recalled that Rossini left the theatre 'as though he had been an indifferent onlooker'. He had, however, been badly shaken by this display of mob violence.

displeasure. But they stayed, remained quiet and allowed the music to continue. That kindness touched me deeply.

HILLER: I can see why!

ROSSINI: To tell the truth, I was the cockiest young man in the world. I loved my parents dearly and I worried until I was well enough established to secure a good life for them. Other than that, I didn't give a damn about anything or anyone. This might have been very wrong. But I couldn't do otherwise. It's how I was made.

HILLER: It is good that it was thus! Otherwise you could not have composed *Il barbiere*. And speaking of that I've heard that Marcellina's aria in Act 2 was not composed by you.[63] Is that so?

ROSSINI: You mean the *aria di sorbetto*?[64] I'm proud to say that I composed it myself. Which reminds me of the story of another *aria di sorbetto* which was rather amusing.

HILLER: Which was that?

ROSSINI: For the opera *Ciro in Babilonia*, I had a terrible *second donna*.[65] Not only was she uglier than is permissible, her voice was beneath contempt. After the most careful testing, I found that she had one note, the B in the middle octave, which wasn't too bad. So I wrote an aria which confined itself to that note; everything else was in the orchestra. The piece was liked and applauded and my one-note soloist was delighted with her triumph.

HILLER: At least your demands were modest. But *Ciro in Babilonia*? I've neither seen nor heard it.[66]

---

63 'Il vecchiotto cerca moglie'. The character is Berta not Marcellina. Hiller is confusing Rossini's *Il barbiere di Siviglia* with Mozart's *Le nozze di Figaro*.

64 A solo number for a minor character designed to be sung when the principal characters are offstage. In Italian theatres it gave ice-cream vendors a chance to trade their wares.

65 Anna Savinelli.

66 *Ciro in Babilonia*, a biblical *dramma con cori*, had its *prima* in Ferrara on 14 March 1812.

ROSSINI: It was one of my fiascos. When I returned to Bologna after its unfortunate premiere, I found myself invited to a picnic. So I went to a confectioner's and ordered a marzipan ship with 'Ciro' on its pennant. The mast was broken, the sails were tattered, and it lay on its side in a sea of cream. It was with great hilarity that the merry company consumed my wreck.

HILLER: But that doesn't prove that your Persian conqueror deserved this fate. These are separate matters. *Zelmira* is one of your least known works and certainly one of your best.

ROSSINI: It had great success in Vienna during my visit there but it requires a superb company of singers. Those we had in Vienna.[67] It was a very beautiful time.

HILLER: Were you happy with the musical resources you had in Vienna?

ROSSINI: The chorus was superb. The orchestra was also very good. All it lacked was power, which can probably be attributed to the hall. Did you know Weigl?[68]

HILLER: I caught a glimpse of him when I was a boy. He was conducting then.

ROSSINI: Indeed. He knew that I had described him as my great adversary. To convince me otherwise, he studied *Zelmira* with an extraordinary care for the orchestral writing. Sometimes I felt like asking him to avoid exaggeration. But I had to concede it went wonderfully. At that time I heard many of my works in German translation, and always with the greatest satisfaction. As I later came to realise, the German language is suited to my music much better than the French.

---

67 *Zelmira* had its *prima* at the San Carlo in Naples on 16 February 1822. It was, however, a commission for Vienna's Kärntnertortheater, where it opened the San Carlo's Viennese season on 13 April 1822.

68 Weigl, Joseph (1766–1846), Austrian composer and conductor. Brought up at the Esterházy court (Haydn was his godfather), he moved to Vienna where as a répétiteur at the Burgtheater he worked with Mozart on the preparation of *Le noʒʒe di Figaro* and *Don Giovanni*. In 1792 he became the theatre's resident composer and Kapellmeister.

Among the singers, I remember the bass Forti as a great talent.[69] Ungher[70] and Sonntag[71] were also beginning their careers then.

HILLER: What you say about German translations of your work doesn't surprise me. Though I wouldn't guarantee the quality of the style, the quality of German prosody, which determines long and short syllables reasonably well, is much closer to Italian than it is to French.

ROSSINI: There have been adaptations of several of my operas which have left me not believing my ears – the matching of text to music was impossible, unbearable. Yet Nourrit,[72] to whom I expressed my annoyance, found everything in perfect order. For myself, I had the impression that no one else was shocked. And since no one is more exacting about such matters than the French, I gave up. Not that my view of the situation changed.[73]

69 Forti, Anton (1790–1859), Austrian baritone. A famously stylish singer and actor, he sang bass, baritone and tenor roles.

70 Unger [Ungher], Karoline (1803–77), Austrian contralto. She made her debut as Tancredi in Vienna in 1821. After being signed by Domenico Barbaja in Naples in 1825, she made much of her Italian career. Rossini engaged her for the Théâtre Italien in Paris in the 1830s. He is said to have described her as possessing 'the ardour of the south, the energy of the north, brazen lungs, a silver voice and a golden talent'.

71 Sontag [Sonntag], Henriette (1806–54), German soprano. Rossini's memory is typically precise. It was after hearing the 17-year-old Sontag in his La donna del lago in Vienna in 1823 that Weber offered her the title role in Euryanthe. She made her Paris debut at the Théâtre Italien as Rosina in 1826. Her first career ended in 1830 when she married a Sicilian diplomat but she returned to the stage in 1850 after her husband lost his position after the revolutions of 1848. She died of cholera while on a visit to Mexico City in 1854. Berlioz was also an admirer, describing her as having 'all the gifts of art and nature'.

72 Nourrit, Adolphe (1802–39), French tenor and pupil of Manuel García. He created leading roles in four of Rossini's Paris operas, including the title role in Le Comte Ory and Arnold in Guillaume Tell.

73 The case of Guillaume Tell confirms that Rossini, like Verdi, was of the opinion that successful translation from French to Italian was well-nigh impossible. The problem centred mainly on verse metres. French and Italian librettists of the time, like French and Italian poets, used different verse forms.

HILLER: French composers are sometimes surpassed by foreigners when it comes to the accurate setting of their language. How beautifully our German Gluck articulates French!

ROSSINI: He would have been in trouble had he not done so, given that declamation is the basis of his art!

HILLER: Maestro, do you believe that poetry and music can arouse *the same interest* at the *same* time?

ROSSINI: If magical sounds have transfixed the listener, the text will always come off worse. But, then, if the music doesn't grip you what then? The text becomes unnecessary, superfluous, distracting even.

6

HILLER: You still have something to say about your childhood, Maestro. After all, you were still only a boy when you began writing operas. How did you come to make your debut in Venice?

ROSSINI: Chance plays a great role in all our lives! At 13 I was hired as a teacher of the harpsichord for the opera season of Senigallia.[74] I found a singer who was not bad, but definitely not the musical type. One day she created a harmonically adventurous cadenza to an aria which clashed with everything. I tried to explain that she must have some regard for the harmonies within the orchestra. I thought she'd taken the point but during the performance she reverted to her old ways and inserted a cadenza which I couldn't help laughing at. The people in the stalls also burst out laughing. The lady was furious and complained to her protector, a rich and respected Venetian with a large estate in Senigallia who ran the town theatre. She complained about my ill-mannered behaviour, claiming that I had incited the audience to laughter. I was summoned before this somewhat severe gentleman who stormed at me, 'If you think you can make fun of the leading lady, I'll have you thrown in jail'. He certainly had the power to do this but I refused to be intimated and things took a different turn. I explained the problem about the harmonies and convinced him of my innocence. So instead of throwing me into jail, he became very fond of me. Finally, he said that once I had reached the point at which I could compose a complete opera, I should approach him and he would invite me to write one.

HILLER: And he kept his word?

---

74 Once famous for its lavish fairs, Senigallia is 30 miles south of Pesaro on Italy's Adriatic coast.

ROSSINI: It is to him that I owe my first commission in Venice. The payment was 200 francs, which at the time was no small sum for me.[75]

HILLER: And that was at the Teatro San Moisè?

ROSSINI: Yes. The theatre has since ceased to exist, which is a great loss for younger Italian composers. You were given short comic operas which involved four or five characters, no chorus and no scene changes. They were works which could be learned quickly; and the impresario had minimal overheads. So it was easy to get a piece staged and to gain some experience. A number of important composers started this way. Nowadays if a young Italian composer wants to create his first opera, he will find it very difficult, unless he has a few thousand francs to invest.

HILLER: What a pity it is that Italians are now so far removed from *opera buffa* in which they have so many wonderful achievements!

ROSSINI: Especially the Neapolitans, who have a special aptitude for this – though their aptitude perhaps lies more in their lively sense of theatre than in any great musical skill. And nowadays the singers are lacking. Handling a dagger every day makes them clumsy. What's needed for comedy is ease and charm.

HILLER: Would you ascribe this taste for the tragic and the pathetic which is prevalent in Italy today to political events?

ROSSINI: I don't know. But I've noticed that if, against the general run of things, a passably good comedy is staged, it still exerts its appeal and audiences have a lot of fun.[76]

HILLER: 'And that is not to be despised!'[77]

---

75 About £720. *La cambiale di matrimonio* (Venice, 1810).

76 *Don Bucefalo* (Milan Conservatory, 1847) by the 19-year-old Antonio Cagnoni (1828–96) was a case in point, as recent revivals in Martina Franca and Wexford have vividly revealed.

77 A quotation from the Comedian in the 'Prelude in the Theatre' from Part 1 of Goethe's *Faust*. The teenage Hiller played for Goethe while studying in Weimar in the 1820s.

7

One day the Maestro suddenly began to sing the start of the finale of Beethoven's Septet, and then a Scherzo by Beethoven.

ROSSINI: Which of the symphonies is that?

HILLER: The *Eroica*.

ROSSINI: So it is. What force, what fire lived within this man! And what treasures his piano sonatas contain! I'm not sure I don't prefer them to the symphonies. There is perhaps even more inspiration there. Did you know Beethoven?

HILLER: As a boy I was fortunate enough to speak with him only weeks before his death.

ROSSINI: When I was in Vienna I was introduced to him by old Carpani. Unfortunately his deafness and my ignorance of German meant that conversation was impossible. Still, I'm glad I saw him, however briefly.[78] And your Weber, he was really something – the way he used the orchestra and the new effects he drew from the instruments! Did he also write symphonies?

HILLER: He tried but they cannot be counted among his happiest achievements. On the other hand, his overtures are among our best-loved orchestral pieces.

ROSSINI: And with good reason, though I don't entirely approve the practice of introducing the work's most beautiful ideas in the overture. When they eventually re-appear, the thrill of novelty has been lost, whilst when they appear in the overture we can only guess at their later significance.[79] But

---

78 Beethoven had read and admired Rossini's musically iconoclastic score for *Il barbiere di Siviglia*. On the other hand, he had no faith in the ability of Italian composers to write serious music. In a later conversation with Wagner, Rossini reported that Beethoven's parting remark to him had been 'Above all, make more Barbers'.

79 Though Rossini did not make a habit of the practice, there are a number of his operas in which themes from the overture are redeployed later in the piece.

Weber had exquisite ideas! How enchanting is the start of the march low on the clarinets in the *Konzertstück*.[80] I am always very pleased to hear that piece.

HILLER: You would have heard it from Liszt, who played it like no other![81]

ROSSINI: Poor Weber. He visited me in Paris on his way to London. He was so weak and ill, it seemed incomprehensible to me how he could undertake such a journey. He told me he hoped to earn a decent sum of money for his family. But he would have been better off looking after himself. The manner in which he approached me was very strange, almost comical.

HILLER: How so?

ROSSINI: It seems that he had once written a newspaper article on – or rather against – *Tancredi*. Because of this he thought it necessary to find out through an acquaintance whether I would see him. I was a young lad of 20 when I wrote *Tancredi*. If I had guessed that a foreign composer was going to write about it, I would have taken it as a badge of honour. For all that, I was no less eager to receive him.

HILLER: Newspaper articles have never worried you much!

ROSSINI: Of course not! When I think of what was written about me during my time in Paris! Even old Berton wrote verses about me, calling me 'Mr Crescendo'.[82] But it all passed without mortal danger! What irritated me was that many of the stories he circulated – stories in which I was given a very particular role to play – were completely untrue. It's something you have to put up with.

80 *Konzertstück* for piano and orchestra, Op. 79.

81 Liszt and Rossini were well acquainted, though Rossini was not in Paris in March 1837 when Liszt played Weber's *Konzertstück* at a packed recital at the Opéra which had been arranged to upstage the pianist Thalberg.

82 Berton, Henri-Montan (1767–1844), French composer, writer, teacher and implacable opponent of Rossini. One of his verses concluded 'Nous n'avons plus de Sacchini/De Grétry, ni de Piccinni;/Nous n'avons plus que Rossini/À la chi-en-lit [havoc], à la chi-en-lit!'.

HILLER: One day you must dictate your autobiography. The details of a life as rich as yours should not be lost. I shall shortly be making my own small contribution to this. You have noticed how I sound you out as though I was an informer for the secret police.

ROSSINI: Continue to question me, dear Ferdinand, as long as it interests you.

HILLER: Povero Maestro! Then you must tell me yet more!

8

ROSSINI: Does Spohr still play the violin?[83]
HILLER: He plays beautifully but only in private recitals.
ROSSINI: I regret that I never had the pleasure of hearing him. Festa, whose quartet playing drew particular acclaim, always spoke of him with great enthusiasm and said he owed his best work to him.[84] Festa was not his pupil but he saw a good deal of him in Naples. He never tired of praising his full sound and magnificent technique.
HILLER: In that respect no one has surpassed him. But what of Paganini?[85] Have you heard him often?
ROSSINI: He was around me more or less constantly for many years. He claimed to follow my star, as he called it. There was barely a place I visited where he didn't arrive as well. He remained by me for whole days and nights while I composed.
HILLER: Was he interesting to talk with?
ROSSINI: He was full of interesting notions. He was an odd bird but what a talent!

83 Spohr, Louis (1784–1859), German composer, violinist and conductor. A follower of Rossini, if not at all times an admirer, he appeared as a solo violinist at the rebuilt San Carlo Theatre in Naples in March 1817.

84 Festa, Giuseppe (1771–1839), violinist, appointed 'Primo Violino Direttore d'Orchestra' to the Royal Theatres in Naples by Domenico Barbaja in 1810. Dubbed 'the emperor of directors', Festa was Europe's most respected (and feared) orchestral leader. Simon Mayr, who wrote six operas for the Naples theatres between 1813 and 1822 and whose skills as an orchestrator were much admired by Rossini, remarked on Festa's ability to make an ensemble of 30 violins, 8 violas, 8 cellos and 12 double-basses play as a single instrument.

85 Paganini, Nicolò (1782–1840), Italian violinist and composer. Rossini and Paganini knew each other well. In Rome in 1821 Paganini conducted the first performance of Rossini's opera Matilde di Shabran. During that same carnival season they devised the song of two beggars, 'Siamo cechi; siamo nati'. The writer Massimo d'Azeglio recalled: 'Rossini and Paganini had to act as the orchestra, strumming two guitars. They decided to dress up as women. Rossini filled out his already abundant form with bundles of straw, looking absolutely inhuman! Paganini, as thin as a door, and with a face that looked like the neck of a violin, appeared twice as thin and loose-limbed when dressed in drag'.

HILLER: A genius!

ROSSINI: You had to listen to him play from a score – with a single glance, he read half a page. Do you know the story of him with Lafont in Milan?[86]

HILLER: It's often talked about in the papers but...

ROSSINI: I was there.[87] Lafont arrived in Milan with the curious preconception that Paganini was a charlatan and that he must have a short contest with him. So he invited Paganini to share his concert in La Scala. Paganini came to me and asked whether he should accept the invitation. 'You must,' I said, 'otherwise people will think you don't have the courage to measure yourself against him.' Lafont sent him the solo part in advance but Paganini would have none of it.[88] He thought a play-through at the orchestral rehearsal would be sufficient. During the rehearsal Paganini played below pitch but in the performance he took the variations Lafont had introduced in rehearsal and repeated them in octaves, thirds and sixths. This so bewildered the poor Frenchman that he didn't play as well as he could. I chided Paganini for his lack of musical loyalty but he merely laughed up his sleeve. Lafont returned to Paris in high fury. As for the Parisians, they continued to think Paganini a charlatan – until later when he played there and was able to persuade them otherwise.

HILLER: Is it true that in his early days Paganini had a fuller sound and played on thicker strings?

ROSSINI: The more difficult the music, particularly where it was multi-voiced, the thinner the strings he used. But his time

86 Lafont, Charles Philippe (1781–1839), French violinist and composer. The most accomplished French violinist of his age, he was famed for the beauty of his tone and the purity, power and grace of his playing.

87 This is doubtful. Rossini was in Naples in March 1816. From what Rossini goes on to say he may at some point have been involved in conducting the negotiations between Paganini and Lafont.

88 Lafont had chosen the *Sinfonia concertante* no.4 in F by one of his former teachers, the French violinist and composer Rodolphe Kreutzer (1766–1831).

of travelling abroad was later, so there may be some truth in what you say. What always amazed me was the speed of the shift from excitement to calm; how the most passionate cantabile could give way to playing of the most daring difficulty. Suddenly his body would stiffen like a robot. At such moments I'm convinced his body became cold.[89]

HILLER: Is there any truth in any of the fantastic tales that are told about his early life?

ROSSINI: None. He spent a long time in the service of the Baciocchi court.[90] He was then dragged around Italy giving concerts. He didn't become rich doing this; Italy's not the country for that.

HILLER: And so he developed a great craving for money.

ROSSINI: His greed was as great as his talent, which wasn't small. When he was earning thousands of francs in Paris, he went to a restaurant with his son and put down two francs for dinner for *both* of them. And on top of that he took home a pear and a piece of bread for the boy's breakfast. He had a strange desire to become a baron. He found a fellow in Germany who could help him but in the end he wasn't prepared to pay the asking price. He was ill for months with rage and frustration.

HILLER: And yet he made Berlioz a truly kingly gift?

ROSSINI: All Paris knows this, so I have to believe it. In reality, I think it impossible.[91]

89 As an old man, Rossini paid tribute to Paganini's art with his 'Un Mot à Paganini', a single-movement Élégie in D for violin and piano (*Péchés de Vieillesse*, vol.ix no.4).

90 In 1797 Felice Baciocchi married Napoleon Bonaparte's younger sister Maria Anna Elisa Bonaparte (1777–1820). The only Napoleon sister to exercise political power, she became Princess of Lucca and Piombino (1805–14) where Paganini was a court musician.

91 Berlioz confirms the story in his *Memoirs*. In December 1838 Paganini, who was already gravely ill, sent instructions that Berlioz should receive a gift of 20,000 francs. It helped pay off Berlioz's debts and made free time during which he began work on *Roméo et Juliette*. The story of the gift was the cause of much speculation in the press. Rossini, who had left Paris two years earlier, would have heard the gossip at second-hand.

HILLER: There are so many amazing things to discuss, dear Maestro. One of the biggest is perhaps that you did not write anything in more than 22 years?[92] How do you cope with all those musical thoughts whirring round in your head?

ROSSINI: [*Laughing.*] You're joking.

HILLER: Not at all. How can you endure not writing?

ROSSINI: Without cause, without stimulation, without the specific need to create a specific work? It never needed much to encourage me to compose, as my operatic output proves. But that's by the by.

HILLER: You often had to work with mediocre texts.

ROSSINI: Just so! In Italy I never had a completed libretto when I started writing. I was composing introductions before the later numbers had been written. Often I was working with poets who were not bad writers but who hadn't the faintest idea about the needs of a musician. As I result I was working for them rather than they for me.

HILLER: But that had its benefits, Maestro!

ROSSINI: Yes, as long as I wasn't in a hurry to compose. When I was under contract to Barbaja in Naples I had to take care of everything: worrying, supervising all the rehearsals. Barbaja wouldn't pay any invoice which I hadn't signed. Meanwhile I was contracted to write two operas a year. Once in a while I would have a vacation and I would take advantage of that.[93] My salary was only 8000 francs a year,[94] though it's

92 'Anything' is an exaggeration. Rossini had written very little only in the preceding eight years. He resumed regular composition in 1857.

93 Only in 1818 and 1819 did Rossini write two operas in the space of 12 months for Barbaja's Teatro San Carlo. With the exception of *Mosè in Egitto* (March 1818) and *Ermione* (March 1819), his Naples operas were written as bespoke commissions for the autumn season. For most of his time in Naples, he used his end-of-year 'vacation' to write new works for Rome (*Il barbiere di Siviglia*, *La Cenerentola*, *Adelaide di Borgogna* and *Matilde di Shabran*) or Milan (*La gazza ladra* and *Bianca e Falliero*).

94 About £14000.

true that I lodged with Barbaja, so there were no domestic expenses to worry about.

HILLER: Barbaja must have been a brilliant man in his way.

ROSSINI: He conducted his business with a certain grandeur. His pride lay in his having the best possible theatre, which he achieved, albeit at vast cost. This he could afford because of the enormous sums he earned from his gaming contracts. His misfortune was his irritability and his vanity. He thought he knew everything better than anyone else, which ruined him for most people. His building projects cost him untold sums. His son inherited only a million.

HILLER: Only a million!

ROSSINI: He could have left 12 million.

HILLER: One ought to shed a tear for the man.

ROSSINI: What a splendid orchestra there was at the San Carlo at that time! Festa was an excellent director. The *finest* orchestra I ever encountered was that of the Paris Opéra.

HILLER: It is still excellent but it never gave me a feeling of *power*.

ROSSINI: The auditorium is too big. I have a particular dislike of theatres that are too large. They kill everything. Not enough importance is placed on the influence of the location. Move the Paris Conservatoire Orchestra in all its glory to the Opéra and it will be unrecognisable.[95]

HILLER: Let us move, dear Maestro, into the salon, where our wives are waiting impatiently. If we stay here much longer, we shall be scolded.

ROSSINI: Then let's go!

95 The Société des Concerts du Conservatoire had been founded in 1828 under the direction of François-Antoine Habeneck (1781–1849), who was also chief conductor of the Paris Opéra during Rossini's residency 1824–29. Henry Chorley described the Conservatoire orchestra, whose size was roughly that of the modern Berlin Philharmonic, as 'a machine in perfect order, and under the guide of experience and intellect – for these are thoroughly personified in M. Habeneck'.

9

One day we talked at length about Cherubini.[96] Rossini, who was intimate with both him and his family, told me of a number of unknown events. They revealed a curious character in which a truly good nature existed under that rough carapace which was often the first thing one encountered.

ROSSINI: It's difficult to know whether in places his music bore the mark of his morose temper, but what a great musician! And the best man you could imagine. Do you know any other composer who so radically transformed his style?

HILLER: His early Italian operas give not the slightest hint that this is the composer who will create *Medée*.[97] But he did not value these pieces. Once, having begged me to look at some of them, he wrote to say they were merely the experiments of a young man barely out of school.

ROSSINI: Yet I had great pleasure one day recalling his *Giulio Sabino*.[98]

HILLER: How was that?

ROSSINI: He wrote the piece for the tenor Babini who later gave me singing lessons. One day after dinner I sat by Cherubini at the piano and sang this piece from his early youth. He barely knew how to control his amazement. Naturally he hadn't anticipated the connection. It brought tears to his eyes.

HILLER: After the passage of some 40 years, it really must have astounded him! And that *you* brought it to him!

96 Cherubini, Luigi (1760–1842), Italian composer who for half a century was a dominant figure in French musical life.

97 *Medée*, Paris, 1797. Brahms considered *Medée* to be 'among the highest peaks of dramatic music'. Maria Callas led a number of important revivals in the 1950s.

98 *Il Giulio Sabino*, London, 1786.

ROSSINI: Did you know old Salieri?[99] And Winter?[100]

HILLER: I knew neither.

ROSSINI: I last saw Winter in Milan where his *Maometto* was being staged.[101] There were some very pleasant things in it. I recall in particular a trio in which an offstage character is given a broadly conceived melody whilst the two onstage characters play out a dramatic duet. It is finely composed and very effective. What was embarrassing about Winter was his unsavoury appearance. He was a very imposing figure but cleanliness was not his strong point.

HILLER: O, no!

ROSSINI: He invited me to lunch one day. A large bowl of meatballs appeared which he proceeded to serve, oriental style, with his fingers. As far I was concerned that was the end of the meal.

HILLER: What a horrible experience. And Salieri? Did you see him in Vienna?

ROSSINI: Certainly. A fine old fellow. At that period he had a passion for composing canons. He would join us for dessert every day.

HILLER: In order to compose canons?

ROSSINI: And to have them sung. My wife and I, along with David and Nozzari,[102] who generally dined with us, formed a very respectable vocal quartet. In the end we became dizzy with this unending steam of canons and begged him to stop.

99 Salieri, Antonio (1750–1825), Italian composer mainly resident in Vienna. He helped effect Rossini's introduction to Beethoven in 1822.

100 Winter, Peter (1754–1825), German composer.

101 *Maometto II*, Milan, 28 January, 1817. Not to be confused with Rossini's *Maometto II* (Naples, 1820) which draws on a different source.

102 Nozzari, Andrea (1775–1832), Italian tenor. A high tenor whose voice took on a more baritonal timbre after an early illness, Nozzari was at the height his powers in Rossini's Naples years.

HILLER: His opera *Axur* was one of my earliest musical memories.[103]

ROSSINI: It contains excellent pieces as do all his works. That said, in his *La grotta di Trofonio* he lags someway behind his librettist. The libretto by the poet Casti is a real masterpiece.[104] Poor Salieri! Has he not been accused of being responsible for the death of Mozart?

HILLER: Nobody believes that.

ROSSINI: No matter: the slander has been given serious currency. After one of our canon sessions, I asked him directly, 'Did you really poison Mozart?'. He stood proudly in front of me and said, 'Look me straight in the face: do I look like a murderer?'. It was certainly not the case.

HILLER: But he may have been jealous of Mozart.

ROSSINI: Very probably. But you must concede that going from jealousy to preparing poisons is highly unlikely.

HILLER: Thank God it's not easily done, otherwise composers would be dying like flies! But since we are talking about these old men, tell me about Simone Mayr of whom I know next to nothing. Did he have great powers of invention?

ROSSINI: It was not so much invention, as the fact that he was perhaps the first Italian composer to show to advantage the dramatic dimension. Also the expansion of instrumental powers. In Italy both he and Paer have been highly influential.

HILLER: I once saw Mayr, when he was an old man, directing a Mass in Verona. Or rather *heard* him, since he drowned out

---

103 *Axur, re d'Dormus*, five-act *dramma tragicomico* to a libretto by Lorenzo Da Ponte after Beaumarchais's *Tarare*, Vienna, 1788.

104 Casti, Giovanni Battista (1724–1803), Italian librettist. *La grotto di Trofonio* (Vienna, 1785) was the first of several important collaborations with Salieri. A rival of Lorenzo da Ponte and often out of favour in Viennese court circles, Casti was very much a professional's professional. His divertimento *Prima la musica, poi le parole* (1785, music by Salieri), which Stefan Zweig later unearthed in the British Museum, became the basis of Richard Strauss's last opera *Capriccio*.

both choir and orchestra with the pounding of the rolled up
sheaf of papers which he used as a baton.

ROSSINI: He was well regarded and had a comprehensive
grasp of technical and academic matters. His *Medea*, which he
composed in his later years in Naples, is an excellent opera.[105]

HILLER: Italian opera has developed so much since Metastasio's day when the musical content of a lyric drama consisted
of two dozen arias and a small chorus.[106]

ROSSINI: We mustn't forget recitative, which the good composers handled beautifully. Important singers of the time often
obtained a greater effect – and won greater acclaim – with
recitatives than with bravura arias. Those bravura arias
should have been the hors d'oeuvres. Their texts were the
problem: pathetic images and the expression of sentiments
which had already been heard a hundred times. Metastasio's
great merit, following in the footsteps of Zeno,[107] was that of
preparing our language for music. He brought into general
use a vocabulary of pleasant-sounding, singable words which
remains a model for all time. Do you know Jommelli's compositions?[108]

HILLER: His sacred works, yes, but not his operas.

ROSSINI: He is the most inspired composer of that time. No
one knew how to write for the voice as he did. His slow
numbers in particular often have a wonderful melodic beauty.

HILLER: But nowadays would they have the same effect?

105 *Medea in Corinto*, Naples, 1813.

106 Metastasio, Pietro (1698–1782), Italian poet and librettist. His 27 *opere serie* libretti were
set by over 300 composers, ranging from Caldara and Handel in the 1730s to Mercadante
and Pacini in the 1820s. Rossini used texts by Metastasio for songs but not for opera.

107 Zeno, Apostolo (1668–1750), Italian poet and librettist.

108 Jommelli, Nicolò (1714–74), Italian composer. By the time of his death, Jommelli was
regarded as one of the great composers of his age. His transformation of Italy's singer-
dominated operatic culture, anticipates the dramatic revolution Rossini himself would later
effect.

ROSSINI: Our artistic forms are certainly changing and that is important. Also no one can sing these pieces any more. There is a quality of breath-control of which only the castrati were capable, partly because of the rigorous training they underwent.

HILLER: If you compare reports of the remarkably virtuosity of those Italian singers with the simplicity of the music composers often wrote for them, it would seem that singers were permitted very different freedoms from those of our own time.

ROSSINI: Certainly in the past opera composers occupied a somewhat subordinate position. For the most part they would draw a broad outline which the singer would fill out at will. That said, men such as Durante,[109] Jomelli and Lotti[110] will always remain great masters.

---

109 Durante, Francesco (1684–1755), Italian composer, based in Naples. He won international acclaim for his sacred music.

110 Lotti, Antonio (c.1667–1740), Italian composer based in Venice.

10

In the summer of 1836 Rossini was in Frankfurt for a week. Felix Mendelssohn was also there and I had the great joy most days of seeing the two men in my family home. One had recently completed his first great work, the other his last.[111] *The agreeable personality of the famous Maestro so won over Mendelssohn that he played what was requested, whether his own compositions or those of other composers. Rossini remembered that all too short visit with great interest. He recalled hearing a good performance of Mendelssohn's Octet in Florence. He then asked me and Mme Pfeifer, a very capable pianist from Paris who was staying in Trouville, to give him a four-handed rendering of Mendelssohn's* Scottish *Symphony.*

ROSSINI: Mendelssohn knew how to treat the smallest motif with sensitivity and spirit. How is it that he didn't write operas? Was not every theatre inviting him?

HILLER: You don't know our German theatres, dear Maestro. They try out works from all eras and nations, from Gluck and Balfe to Verdi. But they leave living German composers to their own devices. The composer can give it a try but it's not easy for any theatre management to commission a piece.[112]

ROSSINI: But if young talents are not encouraged, if they aren't given the chance to gain experience, nothing will come of them!

HILLER: Nothing does. A Beethoven and a Weber might produce a couple of masterpieces but we are as far away as ever from producing a German national opera. Incidentally, I think

---

111 If Hiller is referring to Mendelssohn's *St Paul* (1836) and Rossini's *Guillaume Tell* (1829), the remark is more memorable for its symmetry than its accuracy.

112 The young Mendelssohn did write a number of stage works. Their lack of success can be attributed, in part at least, to the circumstances which Hiller describes.

German composers will always have a strong predilection for the writing of instrumental music.

ROSSINI: They usually begin with instrumental music, which perhaps makes it difficult to switch to the demands of vocal music later on. Germans must strive to be simple whereas, for the Italians, it's hard not to be trivial.

HILLER: You are very severe, Maestro. It's possible that it's more difficult to practise a noble simplicity. On that point, I must return to the regret which I expressed earlier that you did not continue to write for the Opéra after *Guillaume Tell*. You have no intention of writing a *Faust?*

ROSSINI: For a long time it was one of my pet schemes. I had already sketched out a entire scenario with Jouy.[113] It would have been based on Goethe's poem, of course. Then a veritable *Faust* mania broke out in Paris. Every theatre had its own take on *Faust* and that spoiled it for me. There was also the July Revolution when the Paris Opéra, formerly a royal institution, came under private management. My mother had died,[114] and a continued stay in Paris was intolerable to my father who didn't speak French. So I dissolved the contract which required from me four grand operas. I preferred to stay quietly at home in Italy to cheer up my old father in his final years. I had been far away during my poor mother's final hours. That had given me infinite grief and I had a terrible fear that the same thing might happen with my father.

HILLER: So you moved to your home city of Bologna where I met you in 1838 just as you were getting tickets for an open examination concert at the Liceo. You took that institution very much to heart.

113 Jouy, Étienne de (1764–1846), French writer and librettist. He worked with Rossini on a number of projects in Paris in the 1820s, including *Guillaume Tell* for which Jouy was the principal librettist.

114 Anna Rossini died in Bologna on 20 February 1827.

ROSSINI: During my time in Bologna – that's until 1849 – I did everything in my power to help the Liceo. It was the school where I had had my training! It was great fun. I was able to play all manner of music with the young folk who made up the full orchestra. Our playing was often all over the place but it was youthful and fresh and enjoyable.

HILLER: Did you prefer your sojourn in Bologna to the one in Florence?

ROSSINI: Bologna is my true home. It's an informal, comfortable place. Florence is a much more courtly city, which isn't my thing, though I happily recall the kindness the Grand Duke continued to show me.[115]

HILLER: It seems to me, most renowned Maestro, that you were never embarrassed to mingle with the great and the good when the opportunity arose. You even took part in the Congress of Verona![116]

ROSSINI: I accepted an invitation from Prince Metternich who had written me a most kind letter.[117] He wrote that since I was 'the god of harmony', he wanted me to come to a place where there was a serious need for harmony. If it had been possible to achieve that harmony with cantatas, I should certainly have been able to accomplish my mission. I had to compose five cantatas in no time at all: for merchants, for nobility, for the

115 Leopold II (1797–1870), Grand Duke of Tuscany 1824–59. Regarded as a liberal monarch, he was ousted in 1849 but returned to power that same year when the Austrians regained control.

116 The month-long Congress of Verona, which took place in November and early December 1822, ended in failure when Great Britain broke ranks. Though neutral on the question of Austria's control over Italy, the British declined to back Spain in its dispute with its South American colonies; they also indicated a measure of support for the Greeks in their fight for independence.

117 Metternich, Prince Klemens Wenzel von (1773–1859), politician and statesman. He was the Austrian Empire's foreign minister from 1809 to 1821 and Chancellor from 1821 to 1848.

'Festa di Concordia' – and goodness knows what else![118]

HILLER: How did you manage?

ROSSINI: In part, I made use of earlier things, just giving them a new text – even so I could barely finish the work. I remember a chorus in praise of concord in which the word 'alliance' coincided with the most pitiful chromatic sigh. I had no time to change it but I thought I should give Prince Metternich advance warning of this sad stroke of fate!

HILLER: Perhaps he recognised it as the act of some higher force.

ROSSINI: At least he was forced to laugh. The celebration, which took place in the Arena, was extremely beautiful. I have the most vivid memories of it. The only thing that bothered me was that I had to direct my cantata standing directly beneath an enormous statue of Concordia. I spent the whole time worrying that it was about to fall on my head.

HILLER: That would have been the end of concord.

ROSSINI: Merci! But it was a fabulous time. It was there that I met Russia's Tsar Alexander. He and King George IV of England were the most amiable monarchs I encountered.[119] It's hardly possible to describe how charming King George was. And Alexander was a splendid man, truly captivating. After Verona, I travelled to Venice to write *Semiramide*.[120]

---

118 Rossini completed two cantatas for the congress: *La santa alleanza*, which was performed in the Verona Arena on 24 November, and *Il vero omaggio*, which was performed before royalty and high political representatives in the Teatro Filarmonico on 3 December. The aftermath of the congress was far from harmonious when Verona's Chamber of Commerce attempted, unsuccessfully, to take possession of the autograph manuscript and written parts of *Il vero omaggio*, for which it had paid a commissioning fee of 2400 lire (£8800).

119 Rossini was received by King George IV in Brighton on 29 December, 1823 during his visit to England in 1823–24.

120 *Semiramide* had been largely written ahead of the Verona Congress. However, before its *prima* in Venice on 3 February, Rossini also had to oversee the staging of a new Venetian version of *Maometto II* and conduct two further concerts in honour of Metternich, Tsar Alexander and the Emperor of the Austria. The Tsar, he recalled, rewarded him with a diamond-encrusted ring, the Emperor with a polite smile.

There I found myself among more high dignitaries, including, once again, Metternich, who was interested in music and actually knew something about it. Every evening he would turn up to rehearsals at La Fenice. I had the impression that he was happy to get away from his political friends.

HILLER: These colourful tales remind me of the occasion on which you were received by the new governor of Bologna – this was when the Austrians still occupied the Papal States – and ordered to write a new cantata. Apparently you took a well-known patriotic song and sent it up by providing new lyrics.

ROSSINI: There isn't a word of truth in this. These were serious people and I had no desire to jest with them. I never meddled in politics. I was a musician and never wanted to be anything else. I was left in peace. I do, however, take a lively interest in what is happening in the world, especially in the fate of my country. There's a lot that I have experienced and observed.

After a meal I usually smoked a cigar with Rossini. He had only recently taken up the noble art of smoking for health reasons, after giving up snuff for which he had a great passion. Handing me a Regalia cigar one evening, an act of generosity he repeated every day, he told me that the cigar had originally been made for King Ferdinand VII of Spain, from which it took its name.[121] As I contentedly blew forth my cloud of smoke, I suggested that the king was a man of fine taste.

ROSSINI: The king smoked all day long. When I took a short trip to Madrid with Aguado, I had the honour of being presented to him. He received me whilst smoking in the presence of the queen. His appearance was not overly attractive, or even clean. After exchanging a few pleasantries, he kindly offered me a half-smoked cigar. I bowed and thanked him but I declined the offer. 'You are wrong to refuse it' said the queen, quietly and in good Neapolitan.[122] 'It's a favour that is not extended to many people.' 'Your majesty,' I replied in the same manner (I knew her already from her time in Naples). 'In the first place, I don't smoke. And secondly, in the circumstances, I couldn't vouch for the consequences.' She laughed and there were no repercussions following my impudence.

HILLER: It was a demonstration of goodwill. And, in any case, you had your reasons.

ROSSINI: Of far less concern was the favour bestowed on me by the king's brother Francisco. María Cristina had already

121 5⅛" Petit Coronas. By 1855 the Regalia was being marketed by the prestigious Cuban cigar manufacturer H. Upmann.

122 María Cristina (1806–78), daughter of King Francis I of the Two Sicilies. In 1829, aged 23, she married Ferdinand VII, her uncle by both birth and marriage. After Ferdinand's death, she became Regent of Spain (1833–40).

given me to understand that in him I had a most ardent admirer. She advised that I should visit him immediately after my audience with the king. I found him alone with his wife, making music. One of my operas, I seem to recall, lay open on the piano. After a brief conversation, he turned in the kindliest manner and said that he had a special favour to ask. 'Permit me to perform Assur's aria for you, but dramatically.'[123] Somewhat astonished, and not knowing the meaning of this, I sat down to the piano to accompany him. The prince meanwhile retired to the far end of the salon, assumed a theatrical pose, and proceeded to perform the aria with all manner of gestures and effects. I must confess, I'd never experienced anything quite like it.

HILLER: One must envy you, Maestro! You not only have singers like Pasta and Malibran to perform your music but royalty too. But that trip to Madrid also resulted in the composition of the *Stabat mater?*

ROSSINI: I composed it for one of Aguado's friends, a priest.[124] I did it as a favour with no view to publication, so my attitude towards it was only half-serious. When I got tired of it and couldn't finish it on schedule, I had three pieces composed by Tadolini.[125] The great fame of Pergolesi's *Stabat mater* was a huge disincentive when it came to providing a new setting for public performance.[126]

HILLER: Do you rate Pergolesi's *Stabat mater* that highly? I admit I've never heard it. Reading through the score, I found more fine details than a satisfying whole.

123 Assur's mad scene from Act 2 of *Semiramide*.

124 Varela, Manuel Fernández (1772-1834), Archdeacon of Madrid.

125 Tadolini, Giovanni (1789-1872), Italian composer and teacher who, like Rossini, studied with Mattei in Bologna. Tadolini provided six of the 12 movements for Rossini's privately commissioned 1832 version of the *Stabat mater*. The revised version (Paris, 1842) contains none of Tadolini's music.

126 Pergolesi, Giovanni Battista (1710-36), Italian composer. Rossini admired Pergolesi not only for his *Stabat mater* (1736) but for his pioneering comic operas.

ROSSINI: I conducted it on one occasion in Naples where it made a splendid effect. It needs two beautiful voices. They must declaim well and even help out by giving noble expression to the occasional passage of old-fashioned writing. You must also retain the simple instrumentation of the original. It was recently given – I can't remember where – with a large choir and modern orchestration. That's a completely mistaken approach.

HILLER: I have always thought Pergolesi's reputation to be rather exaggerated. It is true he died young. There are also a lot of people who mix him up with Palestrina – people who know as little about Palestrina as they do about Pergolesi! There's also the much talked about *La serva padrona*?[127]

ROSSINI: O, yes. [*He sings a number of themes from the opera.*]

HILLER: There is a sensibility about Pergolesi's compositions which I'm bound to acknowledge. And I must say that with the passing of time I find myself more and more drawn to simplicity of expression. It's strange!

ROSSINI: It is not at all strange. It's a feeling that can only increase.

HILLER: Youth should be the time for such feelings.

ROSSINI: When you're young you love and do things because they are new and unfamiliar. It is through family life and the love of children and the passing of time that the heart develops. You'll see that I am right.

HILLER: I am already willing to believe you, dear Maestro. No one should underestimate the great influence that our life and our surroundings have on us artists.

ROSSINI: I at least have always been extremely dependent on outside influences. The different cities for which I wrote

127 A chamber-scale comic opera or 'intermezzo', scored for strings and continuo, *La serva padrona* was played throughout Europe in the decades following its *prima* in Naples in 1733.

58

inspired me in different ways. I responded to local taste. In Venice they couldn't get enough of my crescendo, so I gave them crescendos galore, even though I had already tired of them. In Naples you could set that aside; it wasn't needed.

HILLER: Have you been to many of performances of your own works simply as a spectator?

ROSSINI: I was quite often behind the scene. In the auditorium, never.

HILLER: Never?

ROSSINI: My pleasure in that was ruined by an experience which I had. One evening in Milan I was going to the home of a friend to enjoy some risotto. It was still quite early and since we were passing La Scala where my *La pietra del paragone* was playing, my host – more or less against my will – led me into the stalls. A trio was just starting. It's one of the best numbers in the opera but my neighbours, far from being delighted, treated me and my music to terrible abuse.[128] They tore the whole thing to pieces. After that I had no wish to repeat the experience. In such a situation no one can take any side but his own.

HILLER: *La pietra del paragone* played a certain role in your life because, if I understand correctly, thanks to that you avoided conscription.[129]

ROSSINI: Certainly, I was destined to become a soldier. Because I owned a house, there was no way out of it. Not that it was much of a house! This 'castle' brought me in about 40 lire a year.[130] However, thanks to the success of the opera, the Milanese commandant was kindly disposed towards me. He

---

128 The Act 2 Trio 'Prima fra voi coll'armi'. Rossini liked the piece well enough to re-use it in *La gazzetta* (Naples, 1816).

129 The Year was 1812.

130 About £150 in rent.

appealed to the Viceroy Eugène. He was away and I was able to continue with more peaceful activities.[131]

HILLER: Though perhaps no less wearing.

ROSSINI: A first night fiasco is not a cannonball. Ours is a profession in which it is possible to grow old.

131 Eugène, Prince Rose de Beaumarchais (1781–1824) was commander of Napoleon's Army of Italy. At the time of Rossini's proposed call-up, the Prince was leading the Italian Fourth Corps at the Battle of Borodino.

One day when I played for Rossini, he begged me as usual to play a couple of fugues by Bach. 'These damned fugues!' he burst out at last in comic fury.

ROSSINI: When I was at the Liceo at Bologna I learnt the overture to Mozart's *The Magic Flute*. I then got it into my head that I would attempt a similar piece. I set to work, wrote a fugal overture, copied it out, and played it. When I heard it, I was so angry at the effect of my bungling I tore it into a thousand pieces in front of my classmates and the audience.

HILLER: You were over hasty, Maestro. The piece would have given you a great deal of fun in later years.

ROSSINI: There are better things to preserve than one's past stupidities!

HILLER: On the subject of fugues, I think of Raimondi who died recently.[132] He must have been a real magician. He wrote an oratorio whose movements can be performed after each other, alongside each other and over each other. Provided there was no muddle, it must have been truly amazing.[133]

ROSSINI: He had great skills in such things and ventured into even more adventurous combinations. He had a bit of luck with one his last operas *Il ventaglio*.[134] When I was in Naples I got him a job in the theatre so he could earn some money. He

132 Raimondi, Pietro (1786–1853), Italian composer.

133 Hiller is referring to Raimondi's trio of oratorios *Putifar*, *Giuseppe* and *Giacobbe*, which could be performed separately or simultaneously. The first simultaneous performance took place in Rome's Teatro Argentina in August 1852 with a combined total of 430 performers. The 65-year-old Raimondi was so overcome with the grandeur of the sound at the work's climax that he fainted.

134 *Il ventaglio* ('The Fan'), *melodramma comico*, Naples, 1831. The success of the opera helped Raimondi secure his position as Counterpoint Master and Director of the Palermo Conservatory, as well as the directorship of the Palermo Opera.

had to supervise and arrange ballet music – a sad occupation for a learned musician. He later found an honourable position at the conservatoire in Palermo. But nowhere did he do well for long.

HILLER: There's a passionate music-lover in Cologne who approached Raimondi after the Rome performance of the oratorios to see if he could acquire a copy of the music. Raimondi asked for a mere 60,000 francs. His success must have unbalanced him.[135]

ROSSINI: I'm not surprised. He never had two pennies to rub together and this was his greatest success.

We were interrupted by a lovely French lady who thanked the Maestro for the many hours of pleasure his music had brought her. To tell the truth, this happened every day but the warmth with which people expressed their feelings was truly touching.

HILLER: Although you are accustomed to such demonstrations, Maestro, the way in which the lady approached you was most agreeable.

ROSSINI: Observations which come from the heart are always agreeable.

HILLER: You must admit that the French have in the highest degree the gift of expressing their reverence for great people in the kindest possible way.

ROSSINI: Certainly. If only they didn't praise me so much and talked less about my work! They can't help themselves, from the most eminent folk down to the concierge. I have yet to meet a Frenchman who does not ask which of my works I prefer. You can imagine how ill-suited I am to participate in such a discussion. They are friendly and appreciative but sometimes they overdo it.

135 Given the costs involved, Raimondi's demand for a copying and performance fee of £200,000 might simply have been an impolite refusal of an unreasonable request.

HILLER: Do you prefer the Italian way?

ROSSINI: The Italians are distinguished by their noble indifference. This, too, you can overdo.

HILLER: You cannot condemn both sides of the Alps, Maestro. There is a proud son of Albion here who told me yesterday with tears in his eyes of the evening he first saw you and heard your music.

ROSSINI: The English have been attentive to me, something which is not readily achieved. The conduct of the Duke of Devonshire was unforgettable.[136]

HILLER: How did he assist you, Maestro?

ROSSINI: During my journey to London I found myself passing through Milan where the Duke was staying. An acquaintance of mine who was about to visit him wouldn't leave me alone until I went too – this despite the fact that my travelling-clothes were not exactly what one would wear to the drawing-room of an English gentleman. The Duke, a great music-lover, overwhelmed me with kindness. We dined cheerfully and after dinner I sang for him.

HILLER: That must have been a bad moment.

ROSSINI: So singers tell me. But I must say that I never sang better or more willingly than after a good dinner. But to return to the Duke. He was not in England during my stay but he provided letters of introduction which were very useful in London.

HILLER: So far everything's as it should be, Maestro.

ROSSINI: Patience, mio caro. Twenty years passed during which I did not see the Duke. Then early one morning I went to the market in Bologna. You must know that nothing equals the Bologna market. You can't imagine the wealth of produce they have there. Strolling through the market was one of my favourite occupations. To my surprise I saw planted in the

136 Cavendish, William, 6th Duke of Devonshire (1790–1858). Known as the 'bachelor duke', he was a reform-minded politician with a wide range of cultural interests.

middle of the square a gentleman calming smoking a cigar. The moment he saw me he raised a friendly hand in greeting. It was the Duke. I told him how pleased I was that we had met, though we would have met anyway since I knew where he was staying and what his movements were. After we had talked for a while, I took him to his hotel and later made my promised visit. 'I remain your debtor,' he said as I was about to leave. 'Our evening in Milan gave me much pleasure but I have not yet had a chance to repay you.' With these words he handed me a beautiful snuffbox. What gave me the most pleasure was not the precious nature of the gift but his extraordinary thoughtfulness. To repay a debt after twenty years in such a way. After all, I had done nothing. It was I who owed the debt.

HILLER: It depends on your point of view. In any case, the behaviour of the duke was gentlemanly, in the best sense of the word. But today we can't talk undisturbed here. There arrives an elegant 'pianist-composer' who has certainly got you in his sights.

ROSSINI: As long as he doesn't want to play a fantasy on themes from my operas. Nothing bores me more than such strumming. And when they've done their worst, you have to thank them for the honour.

The storm which had threatened happily passed the Maestro by.
This incidentally was the last evening Rossini spent in Trouville.
He left the following morning. I accompanied him to his carriage.
Though I was to see him again in Paris in few days' time, I was
saddened nonetheless.

'I expect you for Friday lunch, dear Ferdinand,' he called.
'And for the rest of Friday,' cried Mme Rossini.

I returned home with a feeling, half sad, half pleasant, of having
lived through what for me was a memorable week. I hope that these
— as I see now — all too fragmentary pages of reminiscence convey to
the reader a fair idea of one of the most genial and lovable personal-
ities of this century;[137] a man who among his many outstanding
qualities has the extremely desirable virtue of wishing well to the
writer of these lines.

137 In its obituary notice published in London on 16 November 1868, *The Times* noted
that Rossini had been sought out and courted not only for his fame as a composer but for
his wit, humour, amiability, and goodness. 'With him' *The Times* concluded 'has departed
one of the most remarkable geniuses, and one of the kindliest spirits of the nineteenth
century.'

Index

Aguado, Alejandro Maria, 28
Albani, Emma, 21n
Alexander I, tsar of Russia, 54
Azeglio, Massimo d', 41n

Babini, Matteo, 13, 17, 46
Baciocchi, Felice, 43n
Bach, Johann Sebastian, 9-10, 61
Bach-Gesellschaft
J. S. Bach: Werke, 9n
Baini, Giuseppe, ix, 10
Bakunin, Mikhail, viii
Balfe, Michael, xi, 51
Balzac, Honoré de, 14n
La Peau de chagrin, 14n
Barbaja, Domenico, 18, 34n, 41n, 44-45
Beethoven, Ludwig van, vii, 18, 38, 47n, 51
Piano Concerto No.5, vii
Piano sonatas, 38
Septet, 38
Symphony No 3, *Eroica*, 38
Bellini, Vincenzo, 13n,
Berlioz, Hector, viii, ix
Memoirs, 43n
Roméo et Juliette, 43n
Symphonie Fantastique, viii
Berry, Charles Ferdinand, duc de, xi
Berry, Marie-Caroline, duchesse de, xi
Berton, Henri-Montan, 39

Bollettino del Centro Rossiniano di Studi, x
Bologna, 10-14, 13n, 14n, 15, 22, 26, 33 52-53, 55, 61, 63
Bonaparte, Maria Anna Elisa, 43n
Bordogni, Giulio, 21n
Brahms, Johannes, 46n
Breney, Desle-François, xii

Cagli, Bruno, ix
Cagnoni, Antonio, 37n
   Don Bucefalo, 37n
Callas, Maria, 46n
Carpani, Giuseppe, 23, 23n, 38
Casti, Giovanni Battista, 48
   Grotta di Trofonio, La, 48
   Prima la musica, poi le parole, 48n
Cavendish, William, 6th Duke of Devonshire, 63-64
Charles X, king of France, xi
Cherubini, Luigi, 46
   Giulio Sabino, Il, 46
   Medée, 46
Chopin, Frédéric, viii
Chorley, Henry, 45n
Cimarosa, Domenico, 24-25
   Matrimonio segreto, Il, 24
   Orazi ed i Curiazi, Gli, 24
   Sacrifizio d'Abramo, Il, 25n
   Trame deluse, Le, 25
Civiale, Jean, 3n
Colbran, Isabella, 14n, 15
Congress of Verona (1822), 53-54
Consalvi, Ercole, 25
Crimean war, 2-3, 27
Cristina, Principessa María, 56-57
Cruvelli, Sophie, 18
Cuiller, tailor, 5

Da Ponte, Lorenzo, 48n

IN MEMORIAM

PHILIP GOSSETT

(*b*. New York, 27 September 1941, *d*. Chicago, 12 June 2017)
Scholar, teacher and tireless worker in the cause of opera,
without whom the extraordinary transformation of our knowledge
and understanding of Rossini's work that has taken place during
the fifty years since the 1968 centenary of Rossini's death
could not have happened.

First published 2018 by
Pallas Athene (Publishers) Ltd
Studio 11A, Archway Studios, 25–27 Bickerton Road
London N19 5JT
www.pallasathene.co.uk

@Pallasathenebooks   @Pallas_books

@Pallasathenebooks   @Pallasathene0
issuu

ISBN 978-1-84368-169-4

Designed by Simon Rendall
set in Monotype Fournier
and printed in Great Britain
by TJ International Ltd

Cover image:
Gioachino Rossini
bronze medallion, 1869
4.5 cm diameter
designed by Adolfo Pieroni (1832-75)
collection: Richard Osborne
(photograph by Hugh Gilbert)